CAROL VORDERMAN'S
DETOX RECIPES

WITH ANITA BEAN

CHECK WITH YOUR DOCTOR

Before starting this or any other detox diet programme, you should consult your doctor. In particular this should be done with regard to any allergies you have to any of the foods, drinks, products, supplements or other recommendations contained in this programme. The detox diet may not be suitable for everyone. Pregnant women should be especially careful and ensure that their doctor advises that the detox diet is suitable for them. If you are taking medication or have any medical condition, you should check with your doctor first.

While the authors have made every effort to ensure that the information contained in this book is as accurate and up to date as possible, it is advisory only and should not be used as an alternative to seeking specialist medical advice. The authors and publishers cannot be held responsible for actions that may be taken by a reader as a result of reliance on the information contained in this book, which are taken entirely at the reader's own risk.

Dedication

To everyone who worked on this book.
And to the thousands of people who followed the detox and let me know how much it has changed their lives.

Carol Vorderman

Carol Vorderman
Sole Worldwide Representation
John Miles Organisation
Fax: 01275 810186
Email: john@johnmiles.org.uk

Carol Vorderman was assisted in the writing of this book by **Anita Bean** BSc R.PH Nutr., an award-winning nutritionist, magazine columnist and author of eight top-selling books on food and nutrition.

First published in Great Britain in 2003 by
Virgin Books
Thames Wharf Studios
Rainville Road
London W6 9HA

A catalogue record for the book is available from the British Library.

ISBN 0 7535 0871 0

All photography by David Loftus
Designed by Smith & Gilmour
Printed and bound in Great Britain by The Bath Press, CPI Group

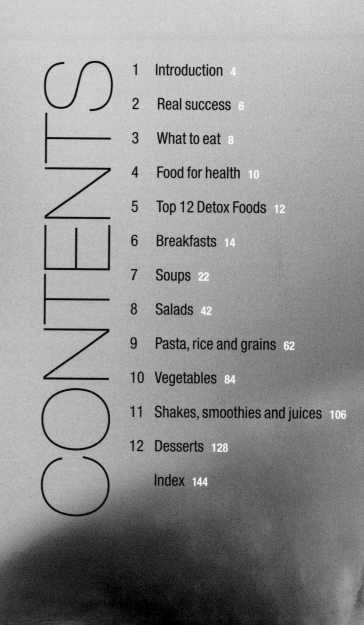

CONTENTS

CHAPTER 1
INTRODUCTION

Both Detox for Life and the Summer Mini Detox have been bestselling books. Hundreds of thousands of people have tried the detox way of eating and loved it. Some have lost a lot of weight, others now feel much healthier, many have found their skin has improved, their eyes sparkle and the cursed cellulite starts to disappear.

There is no doubt that the detox works and thanks to all of you who've written in. I've had thousands of letters from men and women, some with amazing stories of how they've stuck with the detox for a few months and lost stones in weight. Other times, one person at work has suddenly started to slim down and glow, and inspired by this, the rest of the gang has decided to go on the detox together. There are many stories of entire offices sharing recipes and working a rota of cooking and bringing in lunch for each other. They've had a great time and found it easier when everyone has followed it together. Fantastic.

Others, who have previously had health problems, have found their doctors are astonished at the improvement in their blood cholesterol, and love the fact that they feel healthier than they ever have before.

I've particularly enjoyed being stopped in the street and told personal stories of how detoxers are coping. It's quite funny to be followed round a supermarket to be asked if 'this' or 'that' kind of food is allowed. Mind you, there is a downside. I've been out for dinner and just as I've started munching a plate of Italian grub, a detoxer in the restaurant wanders up and wants to know why I'm not feeling guilty!!! Try and get out of that when you've a shovel full of tiramisu almost at your lips. Not easy. But as you

know, the detox isn't something that stops working when you eat a morsel of non-recommended food. As long as you follow the 80/20 rule everything is fine. That means that when you are 'on the detox' as long as you stick to it for at least 80 per cent of the food you eat, then you will get results. When you're maintaining for the rest of the year, that rule changes yet again and that's why in this Detox Recipes book, we've included menus for the 'strict detox' and for 'maintenance'.

Most detoxers follow one lengthy period (maybe three or four weeks) of detoxing and one shorter period (one or two weeks) every year. In between times we eat well, but not strictly. If you've already 'done a detox', then you'll know that your taste buds change for ever. Somehow, after a detox, you really don't fancy the creamy sauce or the chocolate pudding anymore. If you do choose something really rich, then you can only stomach a small portion, which is fine. I really love fish, so I'll eat fish most days, except when I'm on the detox. I can't eat much red meat and I don't want to. I could barely start, let alone finish, a steak nowadays and I'll often choose the vegetarian option on a menu because it tastes nicer. The great thing is I know that I'm getting all the goodness my body needs.

Being of a certain age (43, although I swear my mother lied about my birthday!), I'm more conscious than ever of the need to be healthy. I've recently had an all-over health check and had the thumbs up for everything (and for that I am truly thankful). It was quite a revelation filling in the form and having to think about 'how many times a week do you eat red meat?' 'how many times do you eat chocolate or sweets?' 'how much bread do you eat every day?' and so on. I hadn't thought about it properly for a long time and I found that the answers were interesting (I even got a smile out of the doctor).

It confirmed that the detox programme (and how it changes what I want to eat) has become part of my life. Probably like you, I've tried dozens of different 'diets' but inevitably, even if I managed to lose some weight, the pounds piled back on the moment I stopped. And that was because they often meant eating processed milkshake 'foods', or bizarre mixtures of foods, or only cabbage soup. One in particular recommends an all protein diet to put your body into an unnatural state of ketosis. This diet seems to be about weight control alone. I don't believe that any diet that says 'eating fruit and veg is bad' can be good for you in the long term. What none of these diets do is to educate you to want to eat the right foods. The detox has done that for hundreds of thousands of people. I've found it's now easy to keep the weight off and the health kick going. Having said that, there have been times over the last five years when life has become too stressful and busy and I've completely caved in for about a month. It's amazing how quickly that sluggish feeling returned and how, when I've consciously changed back to eating well, the energy levels come back.

As every year goes by since I was first introduced to the detox, I'm more convinced than ever that this is the best way to eat for a lifetime's health. And it is the lifetime, not the short term, which matters most.

So when I've looked back at all the e-mails and letters you've sent in, one of the questions raised most often has been about recipes for when you're not following the strict detox, so that you can maintain healthy eating for ever. 'More recipes, please?' cropped up time and time again. You want more for the strict detox and you want many more for maintenance too. And I'm not surprised: I understand how tricky it can be. When I did my first ever detox, I think I survived on three recipes. Porridge, baked potatoes and squash with salad and non-wheat pasta with a tomato-based sauce. It got a bit boring after a while, which is why when we wrote Detox For Life we included quite a

few recipes. That helped and so did the recipes in the Summer Mini Detox book, and now we've put together an all-new recipe book with sections for all times of the day and all moods.

The recipes marked D are for those who are on the strict detox: and the recipes marked M are for those who are maintaining. Of course, if you are maintaining, then you can choose any recipe. I'm really pleased with the whole selection we've put together – the food tastes fantastic and I've no doubt the recipes will give you lots of pleasure.

Carol Vorderman

P.S. If you've any comments or stories about how the detox has worked for you then please let me know. Write to me at John Miles Organisation, fax: 01275 810186, or email me at john@johnmiles.org.uk

CHAPTER 2
REAL SUCCESS

Ben Swoyer, 44, finance manager

'For a long time I wanted to lose weight. Despite exercising regularly, my weight had steadily crept up to an unbelievable 16 stone due to my passion for cheese, beer, steaks, barbecued pork and Mexican food. I have always been considered a big eater, something of manly pride. I knew that I needed to change my eating habits to stop me ballooning, but had no clear idea what eating healthily was all about. That is until I went on the detox diet.

My wife bought a copy of Detox for Life and we both started following the diet in January 2003. Beginning the diet was not easy as it took me about two hours to find all the right foods at the supermarket! But now I find shopping really easy. I quickly learned how to drink more water and make delicious smoothies. I have to admit that I did not give up wine completely and sometimes allowed myself the odd pint or two of beer.

I lost about 12lb during the first 28 days and then decided to do it for a further 28 days. I have now lost 20lb, and I feel so much better. I'm fitter and am running faster than ever before. I also enjoy cooking now. I feel like my senses have improved, particularly smell and taste. I sleep better and my allergies seem to have gone. Our kitchen looks fantastic, full of fresh fruits and vegetables. I have also cut down on salt, and I really don't miss meat as much as I thought. That's a big statement from someone who lived in Texas for four years!

The detox diet has changed me for good – I look better, feel better and now have a new appreciation for eating better. Thank you for your diet and a new way of life!'

Lynne Bradley, 57, housewife with three children and one grandchild

'I have arthritis in the top joints of my fingers, which had been very painful, and so I wanted to see whether changing my diet would help. The effect was dramatic. After following the detox diet, I lost nearly a stone, felt great and the pain disappeared from my hands. Apart from the odd twinge, the pain has not returned.

As a keen cook, I make all my own meals. My favourite recipes include soups, vegetable dishes and shortbread. I often adapt traditional recipes, such as salad dressings, pancakes and falafels, so they fit in with the detox rules. I normally make the recipes up for four people and freeze the rest, so I have enough for the month!

The best thing about the detox diet is that the food is lovely. I never feel hungry. And I never get bored with the meals, as there are so many ways to use seasonal vegetables, fruit and grains. It can be hard going out for meals and to parties but I just get back to my normal diet the next day.

My family all eat organic food, where possible, now. I am always aware of what I am eating now and have become a bit of a "preacher" to friends and family!

I recently had my blood cholesterol level checked and the results are great. The good type (HDL) is high and the bad type (LDL) is low, which means I have below-average risk for having a stroke or heart attack. My doctor is full of awe! At 56 and weighing 9½ stone I put my good health all down to my diet. Thank you.'

Lisa Richardson, 34, office manager

'I decided to start the detox after several friends had done it and reported excellent results.

I wanted to lose weight and feel healthier but I was sceptical that the detox diet would work for me. I loved my food too much and imagined that I would be hungry.

But I was wrong. I would have a mango, banana and almond milk smoothie for breakfast (from Detox for Life) and not feel hungry until lunchtime. I loved eating salad with cashew nuts, sunflower seeds and rye bread for lunch. On the few occasions I did feel hungry between meals, a couple of Brazil nuts were enough to stave off the hunger. I found I was able to eat when I was hungry instead of eating by the clock.

My cravings for crisps and chocolate and Mini Cheddars disappeared. The key to beating those cravings was to stock my cupboard with all the right ingredients – no 'naughty' foods allowed – so that I could follow the recipes. My favourite foods were almond milk, avocados, unsalted cashew nuts, and roasted vegetables with pasta and asparagus. I liked the fact that – unlike most weight-loss diets – you don't have to weigh any of the food. I also switched to eating from a smaller plate. Previously I had eaten from a big plate and had seconds. With the detox diet, I found sometimes I could not even clear the small plate!

The hardest thing was giving up cheese and alcohol. I did get headaches at the start due to giving up coffee and diet coke but these soon stopped.

My self-esteem has benefited greatly. After trying to control what I ate for most of my life, I never would have thought a diet plan would have such profound effects. People have noticed how good I look and so far that has encouraged several of my work colleagues to try the plan. They report similar results! I lost 10lb in 28 days and that has spurred me on to continue. A skin rash on my hands has 90% disappeared; my skin is clearer; my breath smells nicer and teeth feel cleaner. I feel full and satisfied for hours after meals. All in all I am much happier now that I am more in control of my eating.'

John Scott, 43, TV Presenter and Stylist, Fashion Expert on ITV's This Morning

'The reason I chose the Detox Diet is because I'm vegetarian – I don't eat any meat, or fish, and I don't have dairy products either, as I'm actually intolerant of those. As a younger person, I suffered from really bad Irritable Bowl Syndrome and since I'm not supposed to have coffee, sugar, chocolate, or things like that, I live with a perpetually grumbly tummy, whereas when I'm on the Detox Diet, there's no problem whatsoever, no sign of that. You feel so much better and you have so much more energy.

Really, I went on the Detox Diet literally to detox, not to diet – I wanted to clear my system out because I was feeling 'fuggy'. And it seemed the perfect one to do. The food itself is good because it's what's in my cupboard. All I have to do is clear out the biscuits and the cakes and the coffee, all the junk food that I do like to eat. As far as the rest of it goes, it's actually the things I'd eat anyway. For example, hummus is my favourite food and you can eat as much hummus as you like!

The first time I did it, I lost two and a half stones. Then I did it six months later and I lost a stone, and each time I do the normal monthly version, I usually lose a stone. But the very first time I did it, I didn't break any rules whatsoever. I just followed the diet, whereas when I do it now, I do cheat a little bit but I still lose weight and I still feel better for it.

From day two it starts working, clearing your system out, so there's not a problem, although I had really, really bad headaches to begin with. Since then the headaches have been nowhere near as bad. Almost on the dot a week later, I woke up in the morning and felt so fantastic. My energy levels were up and my skin was clearer and people were noticing. You might not feel as though you've lost anything – in fact, for the first ten days no weight moved at all – and I know Carol says "Don't weigh yourself", but I was weighing myself and nothing happened for the first week and then suddenly it disappeared from nowhere. I started losing the weight on a regular basis. The thing is I know what it's like to do it now and I know it's worth doing it because you do feel so fabulous at the end of it all.

CHAPTER 3
WHAT TO EAT

ABOUT THE RECIPES

If you enjoyed the meals in the 28-day Detox for Life or the 14-day mini Summer Detox, you will definitely love the recipes we've created for you in this book. They follow the same detox principles, of course, and taste absolutely delicious.

If you are new to the detox diet, the recipes in this book will hopefully inspire you to a new healthy way of eating. They show you how easy it is to prepare healthy meals that fit perfectly into your lifestyle.

Hundreds of thousands of people in the UK have now tried the detox and love it. But many of you have asekd what to do after the first 28 days. And here is the answer. There are two sets of recipes: one set is marked with the symbol D for the strict detox and the other set marked M for maintenance.

The D (detox) recipes in this book follow all the detox rules – no meat, fish, dairy, wheat, sugar or eggs – and are especially rich in vitamins, minerals and other 'detox' nutrients. Use them as part of the detox diet or whenever you want a healthy boost.

The M (maintenance) recipes are a little less strict and may include poultry, fish or low-fat dairy products. They are still well balanced but give you a little more room for manoeuvre. Use them for everyday eating or entertaining.

Some of the detox recipes have a symbol O with optional ingredients that can be included when you are not on a strict detox diet or when you are cooking for other people.

The dishes are simple and quick to prepare and you don't have to be a great cook! The quanitties serve four, but you can adapt them by changing the quantities if you want.

All of the recipes in this book make use of the fantastic fresh produce available from supermarkets, markets and corner shops. There's no need to buy anything from specialist shops. The main thing is to choose the freshest and best-quality foods you can find. Buy seasonal and locally grown produce if you can, visit local markets and if time allows, try to shop little and often for fresh produce so you get the most goodness from them.

Enjoy!

HOW TO MAKE THE DETOX DIET WORK FOR YOU

1. Eat food as close to its natural state as possible
2. Avoid processed foods
3. Drink 6–8 glasses of water daily
4. Eat at least 5 portions of fruit and vegetables each day
5. Eat when you are hungry – never starve
6. Make your skin glow by dry skin brushing daily before bathing

THE DETOX RULES

The detox diet is about eating nutrient-packed fresh food and ditching processed foods, sugar, salt and additives. The vitamins, minerals, antioxidants and fibre in fresh food restore your body to peak health, aid digestion and boost your immunity.

What to eat D

- Fresh fruit
- Vegetables
- Salad
- Unrefined non-wheat cereals – wholegrain (brown) rice, oats, millet, quinoa, rye, buckwheat
- Non-wheat bread – rye bread, wheat-free, pumpernickel
- Non-wheat pasta – corn, millet or rice pasta
- Non-wheat crispbreads – rye, rice cakes, oatcakes
- Water, herbal or fruit tea, pure fruit juice
- Beans, lentils and peas
- Tofu and quorn
- Non-dairy milk – soya, rice, oat, almond or sesame 'milk'
- Nuts – almonds, cashews, hazelnuts, brazils, pecans, peanuts
- Seeds – pumpkin, sunflower, sesame, ground flaxseeds (linseeds)
- Extra virgin olive oil, rapeseed, walnut, flaxseed (linseed) or sesame oil
- Cold-pressed oil blends containing a mixture of omega-3-rich and omega-6-rich oils
- Fresh herbs

Maintenance M

- Low-fat yoghurt and fromage frais
- Skimmed or semi-skimmed milk
- Cottage cheese and other low-fat cheeses
- Wholemeal bread
- Wholegrain breakfast cereals
- Chicken, turkey and lean meat
- White fish and oily fish

What to avoid on a strict detox

- Coffee, tea and other caffeine drinks (including decaffeinated drinks)
- Dairy products – milk, cheese, yoghurt, cream
- Sugar
- Cakes, biscuits, confectionery
- Meat
- Fish
- Eggs
- Wheat bread, pasta, noodles, crackers
- White rice
- Ready meals
- Salt
- Alcohol
- Artificial food additives
- Fried foods
- Artificial sweeteners
- Hydrogenated fats
- Fizzy drinks
- Squashes and cordials

CHAPTER 4
FOOD FOR HEALTH

Detoxing is not about starving yourself, counting calories or obsessively weighing yourself. It's about eating healthily and enjoying tasty meals that help your natural detox system work properly and balance your body. It means limiting the amount of toxins you consume – artificial additives, caffeine, alcohol, salt and sugar – and eating instead nutrient-packed fresh foods. Here are ten good reasons to eat the detox way:

1. **You'll lose excess weight**

2. **Cellulite will diminish**

3. **You'll feel more energetic**

4. **You'll get fewer colds**

5. **You'll get rid of bloating**

6. **Your skin will look smoother**

7. **You'll enjoy better health**

8. **Your hair will shine**

9. **You'll feel calmer**

10. **You can lower blood pressure and bad cholesterol**

CARBOHYDRATES, PROTEIN AND FAT

Your body needs the right proportions of carbohydrates, proteins and good fats to keep healthy. Carbohydrates are an important energy source for your brain as well as your muscles. The recipes in this book feature the fibre-rich carbohydrates – whole grains, wheat-free pasta, fruit, vegetables, beans and low-fat dairy foods – that produce a slower and longer-lasting energy release.

Protein is the building block of your body and is needed to continuously rebuild and repair the tissues. Without enough protein, body maintenance slows down and you'll lose muscle tone. In the detox recipes you can get protein from non-meat sources: beans, lentils, nuts, seeds, soya, tofu, quorn and grains. It is important to eat a variety of these foods so that your body gets what it needs.

It is important to include healthy fats in your daily fats. They help release energy from food, strengthen the immune system and promote healthier skin and hair. They are the unsaturated fats: monounsaturated fats (olive oil and rapeseed oil), omega-3 fats (oily fish, walnuts, pumpkin seeds, flaxseed oil), and omega-6 fats (sunflower oil, nuts and seeds). Try to include one tablespoon of an omega-3-rich oil or a heaped tablespoon of nuts or seeds daily.

VITAMINS, MINERALS AND ANTIOXIDANTS

Your body needs vitamins to convert food into energy, maintain healthy skin, blood and nerves, and to help the immune system work properly. Minerals are needed for healthy bones and teeth, transporting nutrients to cells, balancing body fluids and controlling energy production.

Antioxidant nutrients include vitamins C and E, betacarotene, selenium, zinc and phytonutrients (beneficial plant nutrients). They help to protect the body from the harmful effects of free radicals, boost the immune system and keep you in good health. Diets rich in antioxidants help prevent heart disease, certain cancers, cataracts and premature ageing.

You'll find vitamins, minerals and antioxidants in abundance in fruit, vegetables, beans, lentils, whole grains, nuts and seeds – foods that feature heavily in the detox recipes. Try to eat at least 5 portions of fruit and vegetables daily.

While following a detox diet you may wish to take daily multivitamin/mineral and antioxidant supplements. You may also benefit from a milk thistle supplement, which supports the detoxification processes in the liver. A more detailed explanation of the 28-day detox diet can be found in *Carol Vorderman's Detox for Life*; and a 14-day mini detox diet is featured in *Carol Vorderman's Summer Detox*.

SNACKS

Healthy snacking helps to ward off energy highs and lows. Have a mid-morning and mid-afternoon snack – or when you feel hungry. Try:

- An apple, pear or satsuma
- A bunch of grapes
- A banana
- A plum or apricot
- Vegetable crudités with hummus or avocado dip
- A few cashews, almonds, peanuts or walnuts
- Some raisins or other variety of dried fruit
- A small handful of sunflower, pumpkin or sesame seeds
- A glass of juice
- A smoothie
- Rice cakes, oatcakes or rye crispbreads with peanut butter or hummus

WATER

Drinking plenty of water helps flush toxins from your system. It also rebalances your body fluids, reduces water retention and bloating, prevents constipation and gives you healthier looking skin. Aim to drink 6–8 glasses of water daily. Count herbal and fruit tea, decaffeinated coffee and tea, green tea and fruit juice towards your daily target.

ORGANIC CHOICE

Choosing organic food will go a long way towards reducing your intake of toxins – pesticide residues, antibiotics, nitrates and hormones – but the price of organic food means that it isn't always realistic. If you can't eat organic all the time, just concentrate on organic versions of salads and fruit, especially berries and soft fruit, as these foods are the most heavily sprayed and have the highest pesticide residue content. For other fruits and vegetables, wash them thoroughly in water or remove the peel.

It can be hard to find ready made products in supermarkets which you can eat safe in the knowledge that they're approved for detox and totally natural. I can thoroughly recommend Simply Organics. A small company which makes excellent ranges of 'convenient without compromise' fresh organic soups, sauces and 'Pure and Pronto' ready meals - all of which are organic and many of which are also suitable for detox. Simply Organics ranges are stocked in supermarkets and good independent stores. Call Simply Organic on 0131 4480440 for further information and stockists.

A healthy diet for maintenance should be enjoyable, delicious and also be good for you. Try to stick to the 80/20 rule, which means that you stick to the detox rules around 80% of the time, while the other 20% of the time you are free to enjoy other foods you want.

CHAPTER 5
TOP 12 DETOX FOODS

APPLES

Apples contain vitamin C – a great immune booster – and quercetin, an antioxidant that protects against cancer. Apples are also rich in pectin, a soluble type of fibre that helps lower blood-cholesterol levels and keeps the intestines and bowel working properly.

AVOCADOS

Avocados are rich in vitamin E and alphacarotene, both powerful antioxidants that help prevent furring of the arteries and heart disease. They also contain monounsaturated fat, which lowers blood cholesterol and heart disease risk, as well as the essential omega-6 fats, which promote healthy skin.

BEANS AND LENTILS

Beans and lentils contain a good balance of protein and complex carbohydrates, and provide sustained energy. They are rich in sterols (plant compounds) and soluble fibre, both of which help lower blood cholesterol, as well as B-vitamins, magnesium, zinc and iron.

BROCCOLI

Broccoli along with other cruciferous vegetables – cauliflower, cabbage, Brussels sprouts and spinach – are powerful detoxifiers. They contain phytonutrients called glucosinolates, which can fight cancer, especially of the bowel, breast, lungs and liver.

CARROTS

Carrots are rich in the antioxidants, alphacarotene and betacarotene, which help to protect against lung cancer. These nutrients also help to boost immunity, promote healthier skin and maintain good eyesight.

FENNEL

Fennel helps stimulates the body's natural detoxifying organs, including the liver. It is also good for the digestive system and its high potassium content helps rebalance the body's fluid levels.

GARLIC

Garlic contains allicin, an antioxidant nutrient that helps protect the body from heart disease, high blood pressure, high blood-cholesterol levels and colon cancer. It can also bind with toxins in the body to render them harmless and promote their excretion. It also has antiviral and antibacterial actions.

KIWI FRUIT

Kiwi fruit are super-rich in vitamin C, an antioxidant that helps fight cancer and potentially harmful free radicals. It also boosts the immune system and strengthens the blood vessels.

MANGO

Mangoes are rich in betacarotene and vitamin C, two powerful antioxidants that help ward off colds and reduce the risk of cancer and heart disease. They are also good sources of vitamin E, fibre and potassium.

PUMPKIN SEEDS

Pumpkin seeds and their oil contain a healthy balance of the essential omega-3 and omega-6 oils, which help to protect against heart disease and stroke. Omega-3-rich foods can reduce joint pain and stiffness, improve immunity and promote healthy skin.

STRAWBERRIES

Strawberries are rich in vitamin C. Just five strawberries provide an adult's daily requirement for this vitamin, which not only boosts immunity but also fights free radicals and helps prevent heart disease and cancer. Strawberries are rich in the antioxidant, ellagic acid, which has powerful anticancer effects.

WATERCRESS

Watercress is rich in chlorophyll, a dark green pigment, which helps make healthy blood cells and boosts circulation. It boosts levels of detoxifying enzymes in the liver. Watercress is rich in vitamin C, iron and betacarotene and is good for improving immunity and heart health.

CHAPTER 6
BREAKFASTS

Eating breakfast not only fuels your body for the day but is also good for the brain. Choose from delicious cereal grains, fresh fruit, dried fruit or homemade pancakes to boost your energy and sharpen your concentration. Its been proven that breakfast eaters are healthier, slimmer and happier. So what are you waiting for?

BANANA PORRIDGE WITH HONEY

MAKES 4 SERVINGS

175 G (6 OZ) ROLLED PORRIDGE OATS
250 ML (9 FL OZ) SOYA, RICE, SESAME OR ALMOND MILK
250 ML (9 FL OZ) WATER
1–2 TABLESPOONS (15–30 ML) LINSEED (FLAXSEED) OIL (OPTIONAL)
4 TABLESPOONS (60 ML) RAISINS
2 TABLESPOONS (30 ML) GROUND ALMONDS
1 TABLESPOON (15 ML) TOASTED PUMPKIN SEEDS
2 BANANAS, PEELED AND SLICED
1 TABLESPOON (15 ML) HONEY

Mix the oats, milk and water in a saucepan. Bring to the boil and simmer for 4–5 minutes, stirring frequently.

Stir in the linseed (flaxseed) oil (if using), raisins, almonds and seeds.

Spoon into bowls and serve topped with the sliced banana and honey.

You may substitute skimmed milk for the non-dairy milk.

HEALTH STATISTICS
Oats are rich in soluble fibre – excellent for improving digestion and lowering blood cholesterol – as well as magnesium and zinc. They provide slow-release energy to sustain your energy levels through the morning. The almonds and seeds provide essential fats to help balance hormone levels and promote healthy-looking skin.

MILLET OR RICE PORRIDGE WITH HONEY

MAKES 4 SERVINGS

175 G (6 OZ) MILLET FLAKES
225 ML (9 FL OZ) SOYA, RICE, OAT OR ALMOND MILK
225 ML (9 FL OZ) WATER
A FEW DROPS OF VANILLA EXTRACT, TO TASTE
2 TABLESPOONS (30 ML) GROUND LINSEEDS (FLAXSEEDS)
4 TEASPOONS (20 ML) CLEAR HONEY

Mix the millet, milk and water in a saucepan. Bring to the boil and simmer for 4–5 minutes, stirring continuously.

Stir in the vanilla extract and ground linseeds (flaxseeds). Serve with the honey.

You may substitute skimmed milk for the non-dairy milk.

HEALTH STATISTICS
Millet is a good source of magnesium and iron. The linseeds are super-rich in omega-3 fatty acids, fibre and are excellent for maintaining a healthy gut.

MUESLI WITH FRESH FRUIT

MAKES 4 SERVINGS

175 G (6 OZ) MIXTURE OF OATS, MILLET FLAKES AND RYE FLAKES
300 ML (1/2 PINT) SOYA, RICE, ALMOND OR OAT MILK
2 TABLESPOONS (30 ML) EACH OF TOASTED SUNFLOWER SEEDS
AND PUMPKIN SEEDS
60 G (2 OZ) TOASTED FLAKED ALMONDS
350–400 G (12–14 OZ) FRESH FRUIT, E.G. CHOPPED MANGO, SLICED
BANANAS, STRAWBERRIES, RASPBERRIES OR BLUEBERRIES

Place the cereal flakes in a bowl and pour the milk over them.
Leave to soak for at least 2 hours (preferably overnight) in the fridge.

Stir in the seeds and almonds. Serve in individual bowls, topped
with the fresh fruit.

O **You may substitute skimmed milk for the non-dairy milk.**

D

HEALTH STATISTICS
Oat and rye flakes are rich in
soluble fibre, good for regulating
blood sugar and insulin levels and
reducing cholesterol levels. They
also supply B-vitamins, iron,
magnesium and zinc. The seeds
provide omega-3 and omega-6
fatty acids, to help balance
hormone levels and promote
overall good health. And the
fresh fruit is rich in vitamin C,
betacarotene and fibre.

GRANOLA

MAKES 4 SERVINGS
225 G (8 OZ) OATS
60 G (2 OZ) SUNFLOWER SEEDS
60 G (2OZ) FLAKED ALMONDS
60 G (2 OZ) HAZELNUTS, CRUSHED
2 TABLESPOONS (30 ML) CLEAR HONEY
2 TABLESPOONS (30 ML) RAPESEED OIL
85 ML (3 FL OZ) WATER
1 TEASPOON (5 ML) VANILLA EXTRACT
1 TEASPOON GROUND CINNAMON
1 TEASPOON GROUND GINGER
A PINCH OF GROUND ALLSPICE (OPTIONAL)
85 G (3 OZ) CHOPPED DATES, RAISINS OR APRICOTS (OR A MIXTURE)

Heat the oven to 190 C/ 375 F/ Gas mark 5.

Mix the oats, sunflower seeds, almonds and hazelnuts together in a bowl.

In a separate bowl, combine the honey, oil, water, vanilla and spices. Add to the oat mixture and mix well.

Spread out on a nonstick baking tray and bake in the oven for 30–40 minutes, stirring occasionally until evenly browned.

Cool and then mix in the dried fruit. Store in an airtight container. Serve with skimmed, soya, rice or oat milk, natural yoghurt and/ or fresh fruit.

D

HEALTH STATISTICS
Oats are rich in soluble fibre and provide slow-release energy as well as plenty of B-vitamins and iron. Almonds and hazelnuts both provide protein, calcium, zinc and healthy monounsaturated oils.

DRIED FRUIT COMPOTE WITH VANILLA AND ORANGE

MAKES 4 SERVINGS

1 ORANGE
2 TABLESPOONS (30 ML) ACACIA HONEY
300 ML (½ PINT) WATER
150 ML (5 FL OZ) ORANGE JUICE

1 VANILLA POD, HALVED LENGTHWISE
85 G (3 OZ) DRIED FIGS, HALVED
85 G (3 OZ) DRIED APRICOTS
85 G (3 OZ) PITTED PRUNES

Peel the zest in long strips from the orange with a vegetable peeler and cut into thin julienne strips. Halve the orange and squeeze the juice.

Combine the zest, freshly squeezed juice, honey, water and orange juice in a saucepan.

Scrape the seeds from the vanilla pod with a sharp knife and add to the pan, reserving the pod for another use.

Bring mixture to the boil, stirring until the honey is dissolved, then add the dried fruit and simmer, covered, for about 15 minutes until they become plump and soft. Allow to cool and keep covered in the fridge until you are ready to serve.

HEALTH STATISTICS

Dried fruit is super-rich in soluble fibre, which helps balance blood sugar levels, reduce cholesterol levels and promote healthy digestion. Figs are also rich in calcium and the dried apricots supply betacarotene and iron. Prunes have one of the highest antioxidant scores of all fruits.

MUESLI WITH APPLE AND SULTANAS

MAKES 4 SERVINGS

175 G (6 OZ) MIXTURE OF OATS, MILLET FLAKES AND RYE FLAKES
300 ML (½ PINT) SOYA, RICE, ALMOND OR OAT MILK
2 TABLESPOONS (30 ML) SULTANAS
2 TABLESPOONS (30 ML) MIXTURE OF GROUND LINSEEDS (FLAXSEEDS),
SUNFLOWER AND PUMPKIN SEEDS
2 TABLESPOONS (30 ML) HONEY
2 TABLESPOONS (30 ML) LEMON JUICE
2 APPLES, GRATED

In a large bowl, mix together the oats, milk, sultanas and ground seeds. Cover and leave for at least 2 hours (preferably overnight) in the fridge.

Stir in the honey, lemon juice and grated apple, and then serve.

You may substitute skimmed milk for the non-dairy milk and stir in 3–4 tablespoons of natural bio-yoghurt just before serving.

HEALTH STATISTICS

Oat and rye flakes are rich in soluble fibre, good for regulating blood sugar and insulin levels and reducing cholesterol levels. They also supply B-vitamins, iron, magnesium and zinc. The seed mixture provides a near-perfect balance of omega-3 and omega-6 fatty acids, to help balance hormone levels and promote overall good health. Apples are great intestinal cleansers.

PANCAKES WITH FRESH FRUIT

MAKES 10–12 PANCAKES

PANCAKES:
70 G (2 OZ) PLAIN WHITE FLOUR
70 G (2 OZ) PLAIN WHOLEMEAL FLOUR
2 EGGS
250 ML (8 FL OZ) SOYA, RICE, ALMOND, OAT OR SKIMMED MILK
A LITTLE RAPESEED OIL OR OIL SPRAY FOR FRYING

FILLING:
SLICED BANANAS, SLICED STRAWBERRIES, APPLE PUREE WITH RAISINS, LIGHTLY CRUSHED RASPBERRIES, FROZEN BERRY MIXTURE (THAWED), CHOPPED MANGO, OR SLICED NECTARINES OR PEACHES
NATURAL BIO-YOGHURT, TO SERVE

Place the flours, eggs and milk in a liquidiser and blend to make a smooth batter.

Heat a nonstick frying pan over a high heat. Spray with oil spray or add a few drops of oil. Pour in enough batter to coat the pan thinly and cook for 1–2 minutes until golden brown on the underside.

Turn the pancake and cook the other side for 30–60 seconds.

Turn out on a plate, cover and keep warm while you make the other pancakes.

Serve with any of the suggested fresh fruit fillings and bio-yoghurt.

M

HEALTH STATISTICS
The eggs and milk are good sources of protein. The milk is rich in calcium and the fruit fillings provide vitamin C, betacarotene and fibre.

CHAPTER 7
SOUPS

Health-boosting soups must be one of the easiest ways of supplying your body with vital nutrients. From hearty warming soups like Spicy Parsnip and Root vegetables to cooling summer soups like Gazpacho and Mediterranean Summer vegetable, you'll find delicious soups to revitalise your body and rejuvenate your mind.

VEGETABLE STOCK

MAKES 600 ML (1 PINT)

900 ML (1 $\frac{1}{2}$ PINTS) WATER

2 ONIONS, SLICED

2 CARROTS, ROUGHLY SLICED

2 CELERY STICKS, HALVED

1 LEEK, HALVED

2 BAY LEAVES

2 SPRIGS OF THYME

2 SPRIGS OF PARSLEY

8 BLACK PEPPERCORNS

PINCH OF SEA SALT TO SEASON

Put the water, vegetables, herbs and seasonings in a large saucepan.

Bring to the boil and simmer gently for at least 1 hour. Leave to cool and then strain.

D

Use this stock for making soups, stews and casseroles in any recipes that call for stock. Alternatively, use 4 teaspoons (20 ml) low-sodium vegetable bouillon powder dissolved in 1 litre of hot water.

MEDITERRANEAN SUMMER VEGETABLE SOUP

MAKES 4 SERVINGS

1 TABLESPOON (15 ML) EXTRA VIRGIN OLIVE OIL

1 ONION, THINLY SLICED

2 GARLIC CLOVES, FINELY CHOPPED

1 RED PEPPER, DESEEDED AND SLICED

1 GREEN PEPPER, DESEEDED AND SLICED

2 COURGETTES, TRIMMED AND SLICED

450 G (1 LB) TOMATOES, SKINNED AND QUARTERED

HALF AN AUBERGINE, DICED

1 LITRE (1¾ PINTS) VEGETABLE STOCK OR WATER

A LITTLE LOW-SODIUM SALT, TO TASTE

O 4 TEASPOONS (20 ML) PESTO

Heat the olive oil in a large saucepan. Add the onion and garlic and sauté over a moderate heat for about 5 minutes until it is translucent.

Add the prepared vegetables, stock or water, and then bring to the boil. Simmer for about 25–30 minutes or until the vegetables are tender.

Allow the soup to cool slightly for a couple of minutes. Liquidise the soup using a hand blender or conventional blender. Season to taste with the low-sodium salt.

Serve in individual bowls, adding a teaspoon of pesto to each bowl immediately before serving.

D

HEALTH STATISTICS

This dish is rich in vitamin C (from the tomatoes and peppers), betacarotene and lycopene (both from the tomatoes), a powerful antioxidant that helps to protect against heart disease and several cancers. It is also an excellent source of potassium, good for regulating fluid balance and controlling blood pressure.

ROOT VEGETABLE SOUP

MAKES 4 SERVINGS
1 TABLESPOON (15 ML) EXTRA VIRGIN OLIVE OIL
1 ONION, FINELY SLICED
450 G (1 LB) (APPROX 6) CARROTS, SLICED
225 G (8 OZ) (APPROX 2) PARSNIPS, DICED
225 G (8 OZ) SWEDE, DICED
1 LITRE (1¾ PINTS) VEGETABLE STOCK
1 BAY LEAF
A LITTLE LOW-SODIUM SALT AND FRESHLY GROUND BLACK PEPPER

Heat the olive oil in a heavy-based saucepan over a moderate heat. Add the onion and sauté gently for about 5 minutes until it is translucent.

Add the carrots, parsnips and swede to the pan and mix well. Cook gently over a moderately low heat for 5 minutes, stirring occasionally, until the vegetables soften a little.

Add the stock and bay leaf and bring to the boil. Simmer for 15 minutes or until the vegetables are tender.

Allow the soup to cool slightly for a couple of minutes. Remove and discard the bay leaf. Liquidise the soup using a hand blender or conventional blender. Season to taste with salt and pepper.

D

HEALTH STATISTICS
Carrots are super-rich in betacarotene, a powerful antioxidant that helps prevent cancer, beat premature ageing and promotes healthy skin. All of the vegetables are rich in potassium, the parsnips provide good amounts of vitamin E and swede is a good source of vitamin C.

SPRING VEGETABLE SOUP

MAKES 4 SERVINGS

2 TABLESPOONS (30 ML) EXTRA VIRGIN OLIVE OIL

2 LEEKS, FINELY SLICED

1½ LITRES (2½ PINTS) VEGETABLE STOCK

125 G SMALL WHEAT-FREE PASTA SHAPES

125 G (4 OZ) SUGAR-SNAP PEAS, HALVED LENGTHWAYS

125 G (4 OZ) FINE GREEN BEANS, TOPPED, TAILED AND HALVED

125 G (4 OZ) FROZEN PEAS

2 COURGETTES, TRIMMED AND SLICED

A SMALL HANDFUL OF BASIL LEAVES, ROUGHLY TORN

A LITTLE LOW-SODIUM SALT AND FRESHLY GROUND BLACK PEPPER

Heat the olive oil in a large heavy-based saucepan. Add the leeks and gently sauté for about 10 minutes or until the leeks have softened, but not coloured.

Pour in the stock and bring to the boil. Add the pasta and simmer for 2 minutes.

Add the sugar-snaps and green beans and cook for 1 minute. Add the peas and courgettes and simmer for a further 2 minutes. Stir in the basil and season with low-sodium salt and freshly ground pepper.

0 **Top with shavings of Parmesan cheese.**

D

HEALTH STATISTICS

This soup is a good source of potassium – important for controlling high blood pressure – and the sugar snaps are super-rich in vitamin C. The vegetables also provide folate – useful for reducing the risk of arteriosclerosis – as well as useful amounts of fibre.

PEA AND MINT SOUP

MAKES 4 SERVINGS

2 TABLESPOONS (30 ML) EXTRA VIRGIN OLIVE OIL

1 SMALL ONION, FINELY CHOPPED

450 G (1 LB) FROZEN PETITS POIS

900 ML (1$\frac{1}{2}$ PINTS) VEGETABLE STOCK

A SMALL HANDFUL OF FRESH MINT LEAVES

Heat the olive oil in a large heavy-based saucepan, add the chopped onion and cook over a low heat for 5 minutes until the onion is translucent.

Add the peas, vegetable stock and half of the mint leaves. Cover and simmer for 5 minutes.

Liquidise the soup, using a hand blender or conventional blender, with the remaining mint leaves until smooth.

Reheat gently.

O **Serve with a swirl of natural whole milk or Greek yoghurt.**

D

HEALTH STATISTICS

Peas supply protein as well as carbohydrate. They are also rich in fibre, iron and vitamin C. Mint is an excellent digestive aid as well as a super-rich source of iron, vitamin E and folate.

CALDO VERDE

MAKES 4 SERVINGS
2 TABLESPOONS (30 ML) EXTRA VIRGIN OLIVE OIL
1 LARGE ONION, CHOPPED
2 GARLIC CLOVES, CRUSHED
450 G (1 LB) POTATOES, PEELED AND DICED
1 LITRE (1³/4 PINTS) VEGETABLE STOCK
450 G (1 LB) SAVOY CABBAGE OR SPRING GREENS, FINELY SHREDDED
A LITTLE LOW-SODIUM SALT AND FRESHLY GROUND BLACK PEPPER, TO TASTE

Heat the olive oil in a large heavy-based pan and cook the onion, garlic and potatoes over a moderate heat for about 5 minutes.

Add the stock and shredded cabbage, bring to the boil, and then simmer for 20 minutes until the vegetables are tender.

Remove half of the soup and liquidise using a hand blender or conventional blender. Return to the pan, stir well and reheat for a minute or two until piping hot. Season with salt and black pepper.

D

HEALTH STATISTICS
Savoy cabbage is rich in vitamin C and betacarotene, which are both good immune boosters. The outer green leaves of cabbage contain as much as 50 times the vitamins as inner white ones.

BROCCOLI SOUP

MAKES 4 SERVINGS
450 G (1 LB) BROCCOLI FLORETS
1 ONION, CHOPPED
450 ML (³/4 PINT) VEGETABLE STOCK
450 ML (³/4 PINT) SKIMMED OR NON-DAIRY MILK
2 TEASPOONS (10 ML) CORNFLOUR, BLENDED WITH A LITTLE WATER
A LITTLE LOW-SODIUM SALT AND FRESHLY GROUND BLACK PEPPER TO TASTE
40 G (1¹/2 OZ) TOASTED FLAKED ALMONDS

Place the onion, broccoli and vegetable stock in a saucepan. Bring to the boil and simmer for about 15 minutes until the vegetables are soft.

Liquidise the soup using a hand blender or food processor.

Return to the saucepan with the milk, and then stir in the cornflour blended with a little water. Bring to the boil, stirring, and then simmer gently for a minute or two.

Serve in individual bowls, sprinkling each portion with the toasted almonds.

M

HEALTH STATISTICS
Broccoli is rich in sulphoraphane, a powerful anticancer compound that reduces the risk of cancer of the bowel, stomach, breast and lungs. It's also rich in vitamin C, folate and fibre. This soup is also a good source of protein and calcium (from the milk) and the flaked almonds provide vitamin E, iron, zinc and further calcium.

GAZPACHO

MAKES 4 SERVINGS

675 G (1 1/2 LB) TOMATOES, SKINNED AND QUARTERED
2 GARLIC CLOVES, ROUGHLY SLICED
1 RED PEPPER, DESEEDED AND CUT INTO QUARTERS
1 SMALL RED ONION, ROUGHLY CHOPPED
HALF A CUCUMBER, ROUGHLY CHOPPED
2 TABLESPOONS (30 ML) TOMATO PASTE
1 TEASPOON (5 ML) SUGAR, OR TO TASTE
2 TABLESPOONS (30 ML) EXTRA VIRGIN OLIVE OIL
3 TABLESPOONS (30 ML) SHERRY VINEGAR OR WINE VINEGAR
A LITTLE LOW-SODIUM SALT AND FRESHLY GROUND BLACK
PEPPER, TO TASTE
2 SLICES WHEAT-FREE WHITE BREAD, CRUSTS REMOVED

GARNISH:
HALF A CUCUMBER, FINELY DICED
HALF A RED ONION, FINELY CHOPPED
HALF A GREEN PEPPER, FINELY DICED

Place all of the ingredients in a large bowl and mix together.
Blend in two batches in a food processor or blender. Add a little
cold water – about 150 ml (5 fl oz) – to thin it, if necessary.

Taste the soup and adjust the seasoning with a little more vinegar,
salt, pepper or sugar.

Return to the bowl, cover and chill for at least an hour before
serving. Stir before serving accompanied by individual dishes
of the garnish ingredients.

O **Use ordinary (wheat) bread instead of the wheat-free bread,
if you wish. You may use chopped hard-boiled egg or croutons
to accompany the soup as well.**

D
HEALTH STATISTICS
This soup is super-rich in vitamin
C, a terrific immune booster
that's also good for your skin.
The tomatoes are also rich in
betacarotene and lycopene, both
powerful anticancer nutrients.
As the soup is uncooked, there
is minimal loss of vitamins.

THAI CHICKEN AND COCONUT

MAKES 4 SERVINGS
2 CHICKEN BREASTS CUT INTO STRIPS
ZEST AND JUICE OF 1 LIME
400 ML (14 FL OZ) COCONUT MILK
400 ML (14 FL OZ) HOT CHICKEN OR VEGETABLE STOCK
1 STEM OF LEMON GRASS, CUT INTO STRIPS
2.5 CM (1 IN) FRESH GINGER, PEELED AND GRATED
1 RED CHILLI, FINELY CHOPPED (OPTIONAL)
2 TABLESPOONS (30 ML) CHOPPED FRESH CORIANDER LEAVES

In a shallow dish, sprinkle the lime juice over the chicken pieces, cover and leave to marinate in the fridge for at least 30 minutes.

Place the remaining ingredients in a large saucepan and heat until boiling. Add the chicken pieces and lime juice. Reduce the heat and simmer for 15 minutes.

Ladle into 4 bowls and sprinkle over the coriander leaves.

M

HEALTH STATISTICS
Chicken is rich in protein and B-vitamins. The ginger and chillies stimulate the immune system.

SPICED LENTIL SOUP WITH CARROTS

MAKES 4 SERVINGS
1 TABLESPOON (15 ML) EXTRA VIRGIN OLIVE OIL
1 ONION, CHOPPED
2 GARLIC CLOVES, CRUSHED
1 TEASPOON (5 ML) GROUND CUMIN
1 TEASPOON (5 ML) GROUND CORIANDER
2 CARROTS, SLICED
150 G (5 OZ) RED LENTILS
1 LITRE (1³/₄ PINTS) VEGETABLE STOCK
A LITTLE LOW-SODIUM SALT AND FRESHLY GROUND BLACK
PEPPER TO TASTE
JUICE OF HALF A LEMON

Heat the olive oil in a large saucepan. Add the onion and sauté over a moderate heat for about 5 minutes until soft, stirring occasionally.

Stir in the garlic, cumin and coriander and cook for 1 minute, stirring continuously. Add the carrots, lentils and stock. Bring to the boil and skim off any scum that appears on the surface. Reduce the heat and simmer for about 30–35 minutes until the lentils are very mushy.

Season with salt and black pepper and thin with a little water if necessary. Add the lemon juice before serving.

D

HEALTH STATISTICS
Red lentils contain an excellent balance of protein and complex carbohydrate as well as soluble fibre, iron and B-vitamins. They provide sustained energy, due to the soluble fibre content. The carrots are super-rich in betacarotene, which helps to protect the body from cancer and benefits the skin.

LEEK AND POTATO SOUP

MAKES 4 SERVINGS

1 LITRE (1³/₄ PINTS) VEGETABLE STOCK
3 MEDIUM POTATOES, SCRUBBED AND ROUGHLY CHOPPED
3 LARGE LEEKS, SLICED
1 LARGE CARROT, SLICED
A LITTLE LOW-SODIUM SALT AND FRESHLY GROUND BLACK PEPPER
A SMALL HANDFUL OF CHOPPED FRESH PARSLEY

Place the vegetable stock, potatoes, leeks and carrots in a large saucepan. Bring to the boil, lower the heat, cover and simmer for about 20 minutes until the vegetables are tender.

Remove from the heat and liquidise until smooth using a blender, food processor or a hand blender.

Return to the saucepan to heat through. Season the soup with the low-sodium salt and freshly ground black pepper. Stir in the fresh parsley.

O **Substitute 600 ml (1 pint) skimmed milk for some of the vegetable stock**

D

HEALTH STATISTICS
Leeks are rich in fibre and the green part in particular provides folate, vitamin E, iron, betacarotene and vitamin C. They also contain antioxidants that help to protect the body from cancer and heart disease.

SWEET CORN AND BUTTER BEAN CHOWDER WITH GREEN CHILLI CORN BREAD

MAKES 4 SERVINGS

CHOWDER:
2 TABLESPOONS (30 ML) EXTRA VIRGIN OLIVE OIL
1 ONION, CHOPPED
1 CLOVE GARLIC, CRUSHED
2 POTATOES, PEELED AND DICED
600 ML (1 PINT) VEGETABLE STOCK
600 ML (1 PINT) SKIMMED MILK
420 G (14 OZ) TINNED SWEET CORN, DRAINED
420 G (14 OZ) TINNED BUTTER BEANS, DRAINED
FRESHLY GROUND BLACK PEPPER

CORN BREAD:
175 G (6 OZ) CORN MEAL
1 TABLESPOON (15 ML) BAKING POWDER
1/2 TEASPOON (2.5 ML) LOW-SODIUM SALT
2 EGGS
2 TABLESPOONS (30 ML) RAPESEED OR SUNFLOWER OIL
250 ML (9 FL OZ) SOYA MILK OR YOGHURT
1–2 CANNED OR PICKLED CHILLIES, CHOPPED (ACCORDING TO YOUR TASTE)

Preheat the oven to 180 C/ 350 F/ Gas mark 4.

First make the corn bread. Mix together the corn meal, baking powder and salt in a large bowl. In a separate bowl combine the eggs, oil and soya milk.

Add the wet mixture to the corn meal mixture and mix together. Add the chopped chillies and pour into a lightly oiled 20cm x 20cm baking dish.

Bake for 25 minutes or until the corn bread is coming away from the sides of the dish and it is risen and golden.

While the corn bread is baking, make the chowder.

Heat the olive oil in a large pan. Add the onion and garlic and cook over a moderate heat for 5 minutes.

Add the potatoes and the stock. Bring to the boil, reduce the heat then simmer for 10 minutes. Add the remaining ingredients and simmer for a further 10 minutes, stirring occasionally. Season with freshly ground pepper to taste.

Serve piping hot with the corn bread.

M

HEALTH STATISTICS
This dish provides a perfect balance of protein (from the beans and milk) and complex carbohydrate (from the sweet corn and corn meal). It is rich in fibre, iron and calcium.

PUMPKIN SOUP

MAKES 4 SERVINGS
1 TABLESPOON (15 ML) EXTRA VIRGIN OLIVE OIL
1 ONION, CHOPPED
2.5 CM (1 IN) PIECE FRESH GINGER, PEELED AND GRATED
1 GARLIC CLOVE, CRUSHED
1/2 TEASPOON (2.5 ML) GRATED NUTMEG
1/2 TEASPOON (2.5 ML) GROUND CORIANDER
1 CARROT, SLICED
1 MEDIUM POTATO, PEELED AND CHOPPED
700 G (1 1/2 LB) PUMPKIN FLESH, CHOPPED
600 ML (1 PINT) VEGETABLE STOCK
A LITTLE LOW-SODIUM SALT AND FRESHLY GROUND BLACK PEPPER

Heat the olive oil in a large saucepan, add the onion and sauté over moderate heat for about 5 minutes until it is translucent. Add the ginger, garlic, nutmeg and coriander and cook for a further minute.

Add the prepared vegetables, stir well, cover and continue cooking gently for a further 5 minutes. Add the stock, bring to the boil, reduce the heat and simmer for about 20 minutes or until the vegetables are tender.

Liquidise the soup using a hand blender or conventional blender. Add a little more water or stock if you want a thinner consistency. Season to taste with the low-sodium salt and pepper.

Serve the pumpkin soup with a swirl of Greek yoghurt or crème fraîche.

HEALTH STATISTICS
Pumpkin is super-rich in the phytonutrient, alphacarotene, which helps prevent cancer. It is also rich in vitamin E, betacarotene and vitamin C. Both alpha and betacarotene can be converted in the body to vitamin A.

SPICY PARSNIP SOUP

MAKES 4 SERVINGS
2 TABLESPOONS (30 ML) EXTRA VIRGIN OLIVE OIL
1 ONION, FINELY CHOPPED
1 TEASPOON (5 ML) GROUND CUMIN
1 TEASPOON (5 ML) GROUND CORIANDER
225 G (8 OZ) (APPROX 2) PARSNIPS, PEELED AND SLICED
150 G (5 OZ) SWEDE, PEELED AND ROUGHLY CHOPPED
125 G (4 OZ) TURNIP, PEELED AND ROUGHLY CHOPPED
1 LITRE (1 3/4 PINTS) VEGETABLE STOCK
A LITTLE FRESHLY GRATED NUTMEG
A LITTLE LOW-SODIUM SALT AND FRESHLY GROUND BLACK PEPPER

Heat the olive oil in a heavy-based saucepan over a moderate heat. Add the onion and sauté gently for about 5 minutes until it is translucent. Stir in the spices and continue cooking for 1 minute, stirring continuously.

Add the prepared vegetables and stir to coat in oil. Continue cooking gently over a moderately low heat for 5 minutes in a covered pan until the vegetables soften a little.

Add the stock and bring to the boil. Simmer for about 15 minutes or until the vegetables are tender.

Allow the soup to cool a little. Liquidise the soup using a hand blender, food processor or blender. Season to taste with the nutmeg, low-sodium salt and black pepper.

Stir in 150 ml (5 fl oz) natural bio-yoghurt and heat through, but do not allow the soup to boil.

HEALTH STATISTICS
Parsnips are rich sources of complex carbohydrates – which provide slow-release energy – as well as vitamin E. Parsnips, swede and turnips are all rich in potassium and swede is a good source of vitamin C.

MINESTRONE SOUP

MAKES 4 SERVINGS
1 LITRE (1³/₄ PINTS) VEGETABLE STOCK
1 ONION, CHOPPED
2 GARLIC CLOVES, CRUSHED
2 CARROTS, CHOPPED
1 MEDIUM POTATO, PEELED AND DICED
1 LEEK, TRIMMED AND THINLY SLICED
2 TEASPOONS (10 ML) DRIED BASIL
420 G (14 OZ) TINNED HARICOT, CANNELINI OR FLAGEOLET BEANS
2 SMALL COURGETTES, TRIMMED AND SLICED
125 G (4 OZ) FINE GREEN BEANS
125 G (4OZ) SMALL WHEAT-FREE PASTA SHAPES
400 G (14 OZ) TINNED CHOPPED TOMATOES

Pour the vegetable stock into a large saucepan. Bring to the boil and add the onion, garlic, carrots, potatoes, leeks, basil and haricot beans. Lower the heat, cover and simmer for 15 minutes until the vegetables are tender.

Add the courgettes, green beans, tomatoes and pasta and continue cooking for a further 5 minutes or until the pasta is just cooked (check the cooking instructions on the packet).

Serve the soup hot in individual bowls.

0 **Serve with freshly grated Parmesan cheese**

D

HEALTH STATISTICS
This soup is rich in fibre, potassium, vitamin C (from the tinned tomatoes, leeks and courgettes) and betacarotene (from the carrots). The haricot beans are good sources of protein, complex carbohydrate and soluble fibre.

BUTTERNUT SQUASH SOUP

MAKES 4 SERVINGS
1 MEDIUM BUTTERNUT SQUASH
1 LITRE (1³/₄ PINTS) VEGETABLE STOCK
1 LARGE ONION, CHOPPED
1 SMALL SWEDE, PEELED AND CHOPPED
1 TABLESPOON (15 ML) EXTRA VIRGIN OLIVE OIL

A little low-sodium salt and freshly ground black pepper
Peel the butternut squash and cut the flesh into chunks.

Place the vegetable stock, butternut squash, onion and swede in a large saucepan. Bring to the boil, lower the heat, cover and simmer for about 20 minutes until the vegetables are tender.

Remove from the heat and liquidise with the olive oil until smooth using a blender, food processor or a hand blender.

Return to the saucepan to heat through. Season the soup with the low-sodium salt and freshly ground black pepper.

D

HEALTH STATISTICS
Butternut squash is super-rich in alphacarotene and betacarotene, both powerful antioxidants that help combat premature ageing, heart disease and cancer. It's also a useful source of vitamin C.

CHAPTER 8
SALADS

Sensational salads made with the freshest vegetables
are full of goodness. Raw, lightly grilled, seasonal –
vegetables are terrific sources of vitamins, minerals,
fibre, antioxidants and protective phytonutrients. Bring
out the flavours with fresh aromatic herbs, delicious
dressings, and balsamic vinegar…. healthy eating
has never tasted so good.

GRILLED PEPPER SALAD WITH MINT AND BASIL

MAKES 4 SERVINGS
2 RED PEPPERS
2 YELLOW PEPPERS
2 ORANGE PEPPERS
3 TABLESPOONS (45 ML) EXTRA VIRGIN OLIVE OIL
1 SMALL ONION, FINELY SLICED LENGTHWAYS
GRATED ZEST AND JUICE OF 1 LEMON
HANDFUL OF FRESH MINT, ROUGHLY TORN
HANDFUL OF FRESH BASIL LEAVES, ROUGHLY TORN

Preheat the grill.

Remove the seeds from the peppers and cut them lengthways into wide strips.

Place the vegetables on a baking tray. Drizzle over a little olive oil and turn so that the vegetables are lightly coated in the oil.

Grill the vegetables for around 3 minutes on each side. Set aside to cool.

Place them in a shallow dish. Add the remaining olive oil, onion, lemon zest and juice, mint and basil and mix well. Mix in the onion slices.

Accompany with a green-leaf salad.

0 **Use as a tasty filling for wholemeal baps and sandwiches.**

HEALTH STATISTICS
Peppers are super-rich in vitamin C and the phytochemicals betacryptoxanthin and betacarotene. All are powerful antioxidants that help protect against heart disease. The vitamin C content of this salad boosts immunity and helps to ward off viral infections.

CHICKEN AND MUSHROOM SALAD WITH A SPICY SESAME DRESSING

MAKES 4 SERVINGS

125 G (4 OZ) PACK READY-WASHED SALAD LEAVES
1 CUCUMBER, SLICED DIAGONALLY
A SMALL HANDFUL OF CHOPPED FRESH MINT
4 SKINLESS BONELESS CHICKEN BREASTS
12 SHITAKE MUSHROOMS

DRESSING:
125 ML (4 FL OZ) RICE VINEGAR
1 TABLESPOON (15 ML) DIJON MUSTARD
4 TABLESPOONS (60 ML) RAPESEED OIL
2 TABLESPOONS (30 ML) SESAME OIL
2 TEASPOONS (10 ML) SOY SAUCE
4 SPRING ONIONS, CHOPPED

To make the dressing: Whisk the vinegar and mustard in a bowl. Gradually whisk in both oils, then the soy sauce. Mix in the spring onions.

Place the chicken and mushrooms in a large glass baking dish. Pour half the dressing over and turn to coat. Cover and chill for at least 30 minutes.

Preheat the grill. Remove chicken and mushrooms from marinade and cook under the grill until cooked through, about 4 minutes per side for the chicken, about 2 minutes per side for the mushrooms. Slice the cooked chicken and halve the mushrooms.

Combine the salad leaves, cucumbers and mint in large bowl. Pour enough dressing over salad to coat and toss gently. Transfer to large plate and spoon the chicken slices and mushrooms on top.

M

HEALTH STATISTICS
Chicken is high in protein and low in fat. It also provides B-vitamins. The shitake mushrooms contain compounds that help fight different cancers and stimulate the immune system.

SUMMER SALAD WITH CUMIN AND LIME DRESSING

MAKES 4 SERVINGS

1 LARGE ROMAINE (COS) LETTUCE, TOUGH OUTER LEAVES REMOVED

2 RED PEPPERS, DESEEDED AND DICED

2 CARROTS, GRATED

1 SMALL CUCUMBER, SLICED

4 TOMATOES, QUARTERED

4 SPRING ONIONS, SLICED

A HANDFUL OF VARIOUS HERB LEAVES, E.G. BASIL, FLAT-LEAF PARSLEY, MINT

2 RIPE AVOCADOS

2 TABLESPOONS (30 ML) LIME OR LEMON JUICE

DRESSING:

2 TABLESPOONS (30 ML) LIME JUICE

1/2 TEASPOON (2.5 ML) GROUND CUMIN

1 GARLIC CLOVE, CRUSHED

1/2 TEASPOON HOT PEPPER SAUCE

4 TABLESPOONS (60 ML) EXTRA VIRGIN OLIVE OIL

FRESHLY GROUND BLACK PEPPER, TO TASTE

Cut the lettuce leaves into 1/2-inch pieces and place them in a large bowl. Add the peppers, carrots, cucumber, tomatoes and spring onions.

Halve, peel and pit the avocados. Cut them into 1/4-inch dice and place in a small bowl. Add the lime or lemon juice and toss well (to prevent discolouration). Add the avocados to the other vegetables.

Place the dressing ingredients in a bottle or screw-top glass jar and shake together. Pour over the salad and toss well.

D

HEALTH STATISTICS

This salad is high in fibre and potassium. The romaine lettuce – particularly the darker green outer leaves – contains more betacarotene and iron than most other lettuce varieties. Avocados are rich in vitamin E and heart-healthy monounsaturated oils.

GRILLED SALMON WITH NICOISE SALAD

MAKES 4 SERVINGS
3 EGGS
125 G (4 OZ) FINE GREEN BEANS, TRIMMED AND HALVED
2 'LITTLE GEM' LETTUCES
1 RED ONION, THINLY SLICED
225 G (8 OZ) CHERRY TOMATOES, HALVED
4 TABLESPOONS (60 ML) BLACK OLIVES
4 X 125 G (4 OZ) SALMON STEAKS
1 LEMON, SLICED INTO WEDGES

DRESSING:
3 TABLESPOONS (45 ML) EXTRA VIRGIN OLIVE OIL
1 TABLESPOON (15 ML) LEMON JUICE
1/2 TEASPOON (2.5 ML) DIJON MUSTARD
1 SMALL CLOVE OF GARLIC, CRUSHED

Place the eggs in a saucepan of cold water. Bring to the boil and cook for 5 minutes. Drain and plunge into cold water, then peel.

Steam or boil the green beans for 2 minutes. Drain.

Tear the lettuce into bite-sized pieces and place in a bowl with the onions, tomatoes, olives and green beans.

Heat the grill. Brush the salmon steaks with a little olive oil then cook under the grill for about 2–3 minutes each side.

Toss the salad with the dressing. Divide into 4 bowls. Place a salmon steak on top of each. Slice the eggs into quarters and arrange next to the salmon with the lemon wedges.

M

HEALTH STATISTICS
Salmon is an excellent source of the essential omega-3 fatty acids, vital for controlling blood pressure, balancing hormones and promoting healthy skin. This dish is rich in protein, lycopene – a powerful anticancer phytonutrient – and vitamin C.

ROCKET, TUNA AND WHITE BEAN SALAD

MAKES 4 SERVINGS
125 G (4 OZ) READY-WASHED ROCKET
4 PLUM TOMATOES, QUARTERED
400 G (14 OZ) TINNED HARICOT OR CANNELINI BEANS,
DRAINED AND RINSED
200 G (7 OZ) TIN OF TUNA IN SPRING WATER, DRAINED
4 SPRING ONIONS, CHOPPED INTO 2.5 CM (1 IN) LENGTHS
A HANDFUL OF FRESH PARSLEY, CHOPPED

DRESSING:
2 TABLESPOONS (30 ML) EXTRA VIRGIN OLIVE OIL
1 TABLESPOON (15 ML) LEMON JUICE
1 CLOVE OF GARLIC, FINELY CHOPPED

Place the rocket and tomatoes in a large bowl and mix together. Stir in the beans and the tuna, roughly breaking the tuna up into large flakes. Add the spring onions and parsley.

Shake the olive oil, lemon juice and garlic in a bottle or screw-top glass jar then drizzle over the salad. Toss well and serve.

M

HEALTH STATISTICS
This salad is a good source of protein (from the tuna and beans). The beans are also rich in fibre, magnesium, zinc and iron, while the rocket provides vitamin C, iron and folate.

SWEET CORN AND AVOCADO SALSA

MAKES ABOUT 450 ML (¾ PINT)
200 G (7 OZ) SWEET CORN KERNELS
1 TABLESPOON (15 ML) FINELY DICED RED ONION
HALF A RED PEPPER, DESEEDED AND FINELY DICED
1 LARGE TOMATO, SKINNED, DESEEDED AND FINELY DICED
A SMALL HANDFUL OF FRESH CORIANDER, FINELY CHOPPED
A LITTLE LOW-SODIUM SALT (OPTIONAL) AND FRESHLY GROUND BLACK
PEPPER TO TASTE
1 RIPE AVOCADO, HALVED, PEELED AND DICED
3 TABLESPOONS (45 ML) LIME OR LEMON JUICE

Mix together the sweet corn, onion, red pepper, tomato, fresh coriander, low-sodium salt (if using) and black pepper.

Add the avocado and lime or lemon juice and combine carefully. Check the seasoning, adding a little more lime juice, low-sodium salt or black pepper if necessary.

Chill in the fridge before serving.

D

HEALTH STATISTICS
Sweet corn is rich in the antioxidant zeaxanthin, which helps fight free radicals in the retina. They are also rich in fibre and folic acid. Avocados are super-rich sources of heart-healthy monounsaturated oils as well as vitamin E, folic acid and potassium.

HUMMUS

MAKES 4 SERVINGS

400 G (14 OZ) TINNED CHICKPEAS
2 GARLIC CLOVES, CRUSHED
2 TABLESPOONS (30 ML) EXTRA VIRGIN OLIVE OIL
120 ML (4 FL OZ) TAHINI (SESAME SEED PASTE)
JUICE OF 1 LEMON
2–4 TABLESPOONS (30–60 ML) WATER
A LITTLE LOW-SODIUM SALT AND FRESHLY GROUND BLACK PEPPER
A PINCH OF PAPRIKA OR CAYENNE PEPPER

Drain and rinse the chickpeas. Put them in a food processor or blender with the remaining ingredients, apart from the paprika. Process to a smooth paste.

Add extra water if necessary to give the desired consistency. Adjust the seasoning to taste.

Spoon into a serving dish. Pour over a little olive oil and sprinkle with cayenne or paprika. Chill in the fridge for at least 2 hours before serving.

D

HEALTH STATISTICS
This dip is an excellent source of fibre, protein and iron. Chickpeas also contain fructo-oligosaccharides, a type of fibre that increases the friendly bacteria of the gut and boosts the immune system. Sesame seeds are rich in calcium and magnesium.

GUACAMOLE (AVOCADO DIP)

MAKES 4 SERVINGS

2 RIPE AVOCADOS
2 TABLESPOONS (30 ML) LEMON OR LIME JUICE
HALF A SMALL RED ONION, FINELY CHOPPED
1 GARLIC CLOVE, CRUSHED
2 MEDIUM TOMATOES, SKINNED AND CHOPPED
1 FRESH GREEN CHILLI, DESEEDED AND CHOPPED (OPTIONAL)
2 TABLESPOONS (30 ML) FRESH CORIANDER, FINELY CHOPPED
SEA SALT AND FRESHLY GROUND BLACK PEPPER
CORIANDER SPRIGS TO SERVE

Halve each avocado; remove the stone and scoop out the flesh. Mash the avocado flesh with the lemon or lime juice, using a fork.

Add the remaining ingredients, mixing well. Check the seasoning, adding a little more black pepper or lemon juice if necessary.

Spoon into a serving dish, cover and chill. Garnish with the coriander sprigs before serving.

D

HEALTH STATISTICS
Avocado is super-rich in heart-healthy monounsaturated oils, vitamin E, folic acid and potassium. The tomatoes add vitamin C and the antioxidant, lycopene.

CHAPTER 9
PASTA, RICE AND GRAINS

Pasta is a mainstay in most people's diets so a recipe
book without this delicious food would be unimaginable.
I prefer to use pasta made from corn, rice or millet instead
of the ordinary wheat variety. It's nutritious, quicker to cook
and even tastier. Here, pasta and other healthy grains –
rice, millet, soba noodles and couscous – are combined
with fresh vegetables, delicious sauces, nuts and pulses
to give you plenty of inspiration for main meals.

CREOLE RICE
WITH TUNA

MAKES 4 SERVINGS

2 TABLESPOONS (30 ML) EXTRA VIRGIN OLIVE OIL

1 ONION, CHOPPED

3 PEPPERS (ONE OF EACH COLOUR – RED, YELLOW, GREEN), DESEEDED AND DICED

HALF A CHILLI PEPPER, FINELY CHOPPED (OPTIONAL)

3 LARGE TOMATOES, SKINNED, CHOPPED AND DESEEDED

225 G (8 OZ) LONG-GRAIN RICE

600 ML (1 PINT) VEGETABLE STOCK

1 TEASPOON (5 ML) FRESH CHIVES, CHOPPED

1 TEASPOON (5 ML) FRESH PARSLEY, CHOPPED

A LITTLE LOW-SODIUM SALT AND FRESHLY GROUND BLACK PEPPER, TO TASTE

200 G (7 OZ) TINNED TUNA IN WATER, DRAINED

Heat the olive oil in a heavy-based pan. Add the chopped onion and peppers and cook over a moderate heat for about 5 minutes until the vegetables are just softened.

Stir in the chilli (if using), tomatoes and rice. Stir for 1–2 minutes until the rice is shiny and coated in oil. Add the vegetable stock, bring to the boil then simmer for 25 minutes or until the rice is cooked.

Stir in the chives and parsley and season to taste with salt and pepper.

Crumble the tuna into the rice mixture and heat through for a few minutes. Serve.

Ⓜ
HEALTH STATISTICS
Wholegrain (brown) rice – unlike the white variety – provides fibre, magnesium, phosphorus, thiamin (vitamin B1) and iron. Peppers are rich in vitamin C and other antioxidants while tuna is rich in protein and B-vitamins.

CHICKEN AND RED PEPPER RISOTTO WITH SPINACH

MAKES 4 SERVINGS
1 TABLESPOON (15 ML) EXTRA VIRGIN OLIVE OIL
1 ONION, CHOPPED
1 RED PEPPER, DESEEDED AND DICED
300 G (10 OZ) ARBORIO (RISOTTO) RICE
1.2 LITRES (2 PINTS) HOT CHICKEN OR VEGETABLE STOCK
125 G (4 OZ) COOKED CHICKEN, CHOPPED
125 G (4 OZ) BABY SPINACH LEAVES
A LITTLE LOW-SODIUM SALT AND FRESHLY GROUND BLACK PEPPER

Heat the olive oil in a large heavy-based saucepan. Add the onion and red pepper and cook over a moderate heat for about 5 minutes, until the vegetables have softened. Add the rice and continue cooking and stirring for 1–2 minutes, until the rice is translucent and shiny.

Add a ladle of the hot stock to the rice and cook, stirring constantly, over a low heat until the liquid has been absorbed. Continue adding the stock to the rice a little at a time and stirring until the liquid has been absorbed, for about 17 minutes.

When the rice is almost done, add the chicken and the spinach leaves and stir to mix evenly. Allow to heat through for 2–3 minutes, then adjust the seasoning to taste with low-sodium salt and pepper and serve hot.

M

HEALTH STATISTICS
Both red peppers and spinach are rich in vitamin C, a terrific immunity enhancer and a powerful antioxidant to help protect against cancer. Spinach also provides lots of iron and folate.

SOBA NOODLES WITH STIR-FRIED VEGETABLES

MAKES 4 SERVINGS

225 G (8 OZ) SOBA (BUCKWHEAT) NOODLES
1 TABLESPOON (15 ML) SESAME OIL
2 TABLESPOONS (30 ML) RAPESEED OIL
1 ONION, THINLY SLICED
2 GARLIC CLOVES, CRUSHED
1 LARGE CARROT, CUT INTO MATCHSTICK STRIPS
2 CELERY STALKS, SLICED
225 G (8 OZ) SPRING CABBAGE, SHREDDED
125 G (4 OZ) BEAN SPROUTS
1 TABLESPOON (15 ML) LOW-SODIUM SOY SAUCE
85 G (3 OZ) CASHEW NUTS, TOASTED

Bring a large pan of water to the boil, add the noodles and cook for 2 minutes. Drain and rinse under cold running water. Transfer to a bowl, sprinkle with the sesame oil and stir briefly to coat.

Heat the rapeseed oil in a wok, add the prepared vegetables and stir-fry for 3–5 minutes, stirring frequently. Add the soy sauce, cashews, cooked noodles and combine the ingredients together. Heat through briefly and serve immediately.

HEALTH STATISTICS

Soba noodles – made from buckwheat flour, which is gluten-free – provide slow-release carbohydrates as well as magnesium and iron. The dish is rich in fibre. Spring cabbage is rich in vitamin C and folate – especially the green outer leaves – and the cashews supply protein, zinc and fibre.

CHAPTER 10
VEGETABLES

Vegetables are terrific cleansers and detoxifiers and a powerhouse of immune-enhancing nutrients. Nothing can be more delicious than simply cooked fresh vegetables. Lightly steamed with pan-fried fish, roasted with rosemary Mediterranean-style, grilled with fresh herbs, filled with ricotta, stir-fried with garlic and spices .... the possibilities are endless.

FLORENTINE JACKETS

MAKES 4 SERVINGS
2 BAKING (LARGE) POTATOES
225 G (8 OZ) PACK OF READY-WASHED SPINACH LEAVES
125 G (4 OZ) RICOTTA CHEESE
A LITTLE LOW-SODIUM SALT AND FRESHLY GROUND BLACK PEPPER
FRESHLY GRATED NUTMEG
3–4 TABLESPOONS (45–60 ML) MILK
PREHEAT THE OVEN TO 200 C/ 400 F/ GAS MARK 6.

Scrub the potatoes. Prick with a fork. Place on a baking tray and bake in the oven for 1–1½ hours (depending on the size) until soft when gently pressed.

Place the spinach in a large saucepan with a tablespoon of water. Cover. Wilt over a low heat for a few minutes. Chop roughly and season with the low-sodium salt, black pepper and nutmeg.

Cut the potatoes in halves. Scoop the potato out of the skins and place in a bowl. Mash with the milk.

Mix together the mashed potato, spinach and ricotta cheese.

Spoon the mixture back into the potato skins. Place on the baking sheet and return to the oven for 15 minutes until piping hot.

HEALTH STATISTICS
Spinach is an excellent source of iron, betacarotene, folate, vitamin E and vitamin C. It also contains powerful antioxidants such as lutein, which helps to reduce the risk of cancer. Keeping the cooking time short preserves the vitamin C and folate content.

FISH STEW WITH FENNEL AND TOMATOES

MAKES 4 SERVINGS
2 TABLESPOONS (30 ML) EXTRA VIRGIN OLIVE OIL
1 FENNEL BULB, FINELY SLICED
1 GARLIC CLOVE, CRUSHED
500 ML (16 FL OZ) FISH OR VEGETABLE STOCK
800 G (18 OZ) TINNED CHOPPED TOMATOES
250 G (9 OZ) CHERRY TOMATOES, HALVED
A LITTLE LOW-SODIUM SALT AND FRESHLY GROUND BLACK PEPPER
450 G (1 LB) MONKFISH FILLET, CUT INTO 4 CM CHUNKS
1 TABLESPOON (15 ML) CHOPPED CHIVES

Heat the olive oil in a large pan, add the fennel and cook over a moderate heat for 5 minutes. Add the garlic and cook for a further minute.

Stir in the stock and tinned tomatoes, bring to the boil and simmer gently for 5 minutes.

Add the cherry tomatoes and cook for a further 5 minutes. Season with low-sodium salt and freshly ground pepper.

Add the monkfish, cover and cook for approximately 5 minutes or until the fish is cooked. Serve the stew in 4 individual bowls and garnish with the chopped chives.

M

HEALTH STATISTICS
This dish is rich in protein and B-vitamins (from the fish). Fennel provides folate and potassium and the tomatoes are rich in vitamin C and lycopene, a powerful antioxidant nutrient that helps fight cancer.

RATATOUILLE WITH RED KIDNEY BEANS

MAKES 4 SERVINGS
2 TABLESPOONS (30 ML) EXTRA VIRGIN OLIVE OIL
1 ONION, CHOPPED
1 EACH OF RED, YELLOW AND GREEN PEPPERS, DESEEDED AND SLICED
2 CLOVES OF GARLIC, CRUSHED
2 COURGETTES, TRIMMED AND SLICED
1 AUBERGINE, DICED
700 G (1 1/2 LB) TOMATOES, SKINNED AND CHOPPED
(OR USE 400 G/ 14 OZ TINNED TOMATOES)
420 G (14 OZ) TINNED RED KIDNEY BEANS, DRAINED
175 G (6 OZ) GREEN BEANS, TRIMMED AND HALVED
A LITTLE LOW-SODIUM SALT AND FRESHLY GROUND BLACK PEPPER
2 TABLESPOONS (30 ML) BASIL LEAVES OR CHOPPED FRESH PARSLEY

Heat the oil in a large saucepan. Add the chopped onion and peppers and cook gently for 5 minutes.

Add the garlic, courgettes, aubergines, tomatoes, red kidney beans and green beans. Stir then cover and cook over a low heat for 20–25 minutes until all the vegetables are tender.

Season to taste with low-sodium salt and freshly ground black pepper and stir in the fresh herbs. Serve hot or cold.

D

HEALTH STATISTICS
This dish is super-rich in antioxidant nutrients: vitamin C (from the peppers and green beans), nasuin (from the aubergine), lycopene (from the tomatoes) and quercetin (from the onions). The red kidney beans provide plenty of soluble fibre, protein and iron.

CHAPTER 11
SHAKES, SMOOTHIES AND JUICES

Making smoothies, shakes and juices is a really easy
way to meet your five a day target for fruit and vegetables.
Packed with vital nutrients, they really do your body, mind
and skin good. Drinks made from fresh ingredients help
energise your body, detox your system, revitalise your
senses and de-stress your mind.

SMOOTHIES

- For best taste and nutritional value, choose ripe fruit.

- Remove thick peel (e.g. from bananas), stones (e.g. from peaches) and hulls (e.g. from strawberries) and cut the flesh into large chunks.

- You may substitute frozen fruit – such as raspberries – for fresh fruit

- If your blender crushes ice, start with ice cubes blended to a 'snow' followed by the fruit. Otherwise, crush the ice before putting it into a blender.

- Add ingredients to the blender beginning with liquids and ending with solids.

- Add more or less juice or water to your smoothie, according to your own preferences, to make a thinner or thicker drink.

MELON AND MINT SMOOTHIE

[SEE PAGE 109 FOR RECIPE PHOTO]
A CUPFUL OF CRUSHED ICE
1 GENEROUS SLICE HONEYDEW MELON
85 ML (3 FL OZ) GRAPE OR APPLE JUICE
1–2 TEASPOONS (5–10 ML) LEMON JUICE
120 ML (4 FL OZ) NATURAL YOGHURT
1 TABLESPOON (15 ML) CHOPPED MINT LEAVES

Place the ice, melon, fruit juice, lemon juice, yoghurt and mint in a smoothie maker, blender or food processor and process until slushy. Serve immediately.

HEALTH STATISTICS
This refreshing smoothie is rich in potassium, vitamin C, calcium and protein. It has natural diuretic properties, helping reduce water retention.

APRICOT AND MANGO SMOOTHIE

4 APRICOTS, STONES REMOVED
HALF A MANGO, PEELED, STONE REMOVED AND CHOPPED
1 BANANA
150 ML (5 FL OZ) APPLE JUICE
A LARGE CUPFUL OF CRUSHED ICE

Place the ingredients in a smoothie maker, blender or food processor and blend until smooth. Serve immediately.

D

HEALTH STATISTICS
Apricots and mangoes are super-rich in betacarotene, a powerful antioxidant nutrient that helps combat cancer and also benefits the skin. The smoothie also provides fibre, potassium and vitamin B6.

STRAWBERRY AND BANANA SMOOTHIE

MAKES 2 DRINKS
250 ML (8 FL OZ) ORANGE JUICE
125 G (4 OZ) STRAWBERRIES
2 BANANAS, FROZEN AND SLICED *

Place the orange juice, strawberries and frozen banana slices in a smoothie maker, blender or food processor and process until smooth and thick. Serve immediately.

* Use frozen bananas instead of adding ice cubes to the drinks. Peel bananas, place in a plastic bag and freeze.

D

HEALTH STATISTICS
This smoothie is super-rich in vitamin C, potassium, vitamin B6 and fibre.

STRAWBERRY AND PINEAPPLE SMOOTHIE

MAKES 2 DRINKS
125 G (4 OZ) STRAWBERRIES, HULLED
HALF A PEAR, PEELED, CORED AND ROUGHLY CHOPPED
A QUARTER OF A PINEAPPLE, CORED AND CHOPPED
125 ML (4 FL OZ) FRESH ORANGE JUICE
A CUPFUL OF CRUSHED ICE

Place the ingredients in a smoothie maker, blender or food processor and blend until smooth and frothy. Serve immediately.

D

HEALTH STATISTICS
Strawberries and orange juice are both super-rich sources of vitamin C. The pineapple provides fibre and potassium.

RASPBERRY AND PINK GRAPEFRUIT SMOOTHIE

MAKES 2 DRINKS
225 G (8 OZ) RASPBERRIES
300 ML (1/2 PINT) PINK GRAPEFRUIT JUICE
1 BANANA
A LITTLE HONEY, TO TASTE

If you don't mind the small seeds, blend the raspberries, half the grapefruit juice, banana and honey in a smoothie maker, blender or food processor and blend until smooth. Alternatively, juice the fruit in a juice extractor. Add the remaining grapefruit juice, adjusting to your preferred consistency. Serve in chilled glasses immediately.

D

HEALTH STATISTICS
This smoothie is a terrific source of vitamin C and antioxidant nutrients. It is also a great detoxifier, stimulating the function of the liver and digestive system.

STRAWBERRY, LYCHEE AND WATERMELON SMOOTHIE

MAKES 2 DRINKS
A HANDFUL OF CRUSHED ICE
JUICE AND ZEST OF 1 LIME
85 G (3 OZ) STRAWBERRIES
6 FRESH OR CANNED LYCHEES, STONES REMOVED
HALF A MANGO, PEELED AND ROUGHLY CHOPPED
A QUARTER OF A WATERMELON, PEELED AND CHOPPED
1 BANANA, PEELED AND ROUGHLY CHOPPED

Place the ice and fruit in a smoothie maker, blender or food processor and blend until smooth. Serve in chilled glasses immediately.

D

HEALTH STATISTICS
Strawberries and lime juice are super-rich in vitamin C; the mango and watermelon are packed with betacarotene and the watermelon also provides lots of the antioxidant nutrient, lycopene.

PINEAPPLE AND COCONUT SMOOTHIE

HALF A PINEAPPLE
125 ML (4 FL OZ) COCONUT MILK
1 BANANA
150 ML (5 FL OZ) PINEAPPLE JUICE
A CUPFUL OF CRUSHED ICE

Place the ingredients in a smoothie maker, blender or food processor and blend until smooth. Serve immediately.

D

HEALTH STATISTICS
This smoothie is rich in fibre, potassium and vitamin C.

NECTARINE AND BLUEBERRY SMOOTHIE

MAKES 2 DRINKS
2 NECTARINES, HALVED, STONED AND CUT INTO CHUNKS
125 G (4 OZ) BLUEBERRIES
250 ML (9 FL OZ) APPLE JUICE
A CUPFUL OF CRUSHED ICE

Place the prepared fruit, apple juice and ice in a smoothie maker, blender or food processor and blend until smooth. Serve in chilled glasses immediately.

D
HEALTH STATISTICS
Nectarines are rich in betacarotene and vitamin C. Blueberries are super-rich sources of immunity-boosting vitamin C and antioxidants called anthocyanins.

STRAWBERRY AND KIWI FRUIT SMOOTHIE

MAKES 2 DRINKS
A CUPFUL OF CRUSHED ICE
125 G (4 OZ) STRAWBERRIES
1 KIWI FRUIT
1 BANANA
150 ML (5 FL OZ) APPLE JUICE
1 TABLESPOON (15 ML) LINSEEDS (GROUND)

Place the ice, strawberries, kiwi fruit, banana and apple juice in the goblet of a smoothie maker, blender or food processor and process until smooth. Add the ground linseeds and blend until well combined. Serve immediately.

D
HEALTH STATISTICS
Vitamin C-rich summer fruits will boost your energy levels. The linseeds in this drink are rich in heart-healthy omega-3 oils and are, themselves, powerful intestinal cleansers.

JUICES

TOP TIPS

- Wash the fruit and vegetables. Trim them if necessary, stone the fruit and remove any thick peel. Cut them into manageable pieces.

- You can put most parts of the produce into the juicer, except hard skins (e.g. citrus peel, banana peel, etc.) and stones (e.g. from avocados, peaches, apricots, etc.)

- Choose fruit that is ripe yet quite firm. Avoid overripe or very soft fruit as these do not pass through the juice extractor well.

- Drink juices as soon as possible after preparation. Once they are left to stand, they start losing nutrients through oxidation.

- Dilute juices with a little water according to your taste preference.

BLUEBERRY AND BLACKBERRY

MAKES 2 DRINKS
125 G (4 OZ) BLUEBERRIES
2 APPLES CUT INTO QUARTERS
350 G (12 OZ) BLACKBERRIES

Using a juice extractor, juice all the ingredients, pour into a glass and serve immediately.

D

HEALTH STATISTICS
Blueberries and blackberries contain vitamin C as well as powerful antioxidants, which boost immunity and protect the body from illness.

ORANGE, MELON AND NECTARINE

MAKES 2 DRINKS
2 ORANGES
HALF A CANTALOUPE MELON
1 NECTARINE

Using a juice extractor, juice all the ingredients, pour into a glass and serve immediately.

D

HEALTH STATISTICS
This drink is a super immune booster. Oranges, melon and nectarine all provide vitamin C while the cantaloupe melon is rich in betacarotene.

TOMATO AND CELERY

MAKES 2 DRINKS
6 TOMATOES
2 CELERY STICKS
HALF A RED PEPPER

Using a juice extractor, juice all the ingredients, pour into a glass and serve immediately.

D

HEALTH STATISTICS
Tomatoes are super-rich in lycopene, which can help combat several cancers, as well as vitamin C. The red pepper boosts the vitamin C content further and the celery adds to the cleansing properties of this juice

GREENS AND PINEAPPLE

MAKES 2 DRINKS
1 BUNCH OF WATERCRESS
4 BROCCOLI SPEARS
1 BUNCH OF PARSLEY
1 CELERY STICK
HALF A PINEAPPLE

Using a juice extractor, juice all the ingredients, pour into a glass and serve immediately.

D

HEALTH STATISTICS
This juice is super-rich in vitamin C, betacarotene, iron, magnesium, folic acid and calcium. It stimulates detoxification and is also a great immune booster.

CUCUMBER AND MINT

MAKES 2 DRINKS
1 CUCUMBER
1 APPLE
1 PEAR
4 SPRIGS OF FRESH MINT

Using a juice extractor, juice all the ingredients, pour into a glass and serve immediately.

D

HEALTH STATISTICS
This juice is a wonderful cleanser. Cucumber is a good diuretic, helping reduce water retention. This juice provides potassium, vitamin C and antioxidant nutrients.

GRAPE AND CELERY

MAKES 2 DRINKS
225 G (8 OZ) GREEN SEEDLESS GRAPES
4 CELERY STICKS

Using a juice extractor, juice all the ingredients, pour into a glass and serve immediately.

D

HEALTH STATISTICS
This cleansing juice also benefits the skin and immune system. It provides antioxidant nutrients, potassium and vitamin C.

CARROT AND PEPPERS

MAKES 2 DRINKS
2 CARROTS
1 RED PEPPER
1 YELLOW PEPPER

Using a juice extractor, juice all the ingredients, pour into a glass and serve immediately.

D

HEALTH STATISTICS
Carrots and peppers are super-rich in betacarotene, a powerful antioxidant that helps prevent cancer. Peppers are also highly concentrated in immunity-boosting vitamin C.

CARROT, BEETROOT AND CELERY

MAKES 2 DRINKS
2 CARROTS
1 APPLE
HALF AN ORANGE
A QUARTER OF A BEETROOT
2 CELERY STICKS

Using a juice extractor, juice all the ingredients, pour into a glass and serve immediately.

D

HEALTH STATISTICS
This juice has terrific cleansing properties. It is rich in betacarotene, vitamin C, potassium and antioxidant nutrients.

APPLE, CARROT AND GINGER

MAKES 2 DRINKS
3 APPLES
2 CARROTS
1 CM (1/2 IN) PIECE FRESH GINGER ROOT

Using a juice extractor, juice all the ingredients, pour into a glass and serve immediately.

D

HEALTH STATISTICS
Apples, carrots and ginger are all good 'cleansers', stimulating the liver and intestines. Carrots are rich in betacarotene, and apples provide the anticancer nutrient, quercetin.

APPLE, ORANGE AND LIME

MAKES 2 DRINKS
3 APPLES
1 ORANGE
HALF A LIME

Using a juice extractor, juice all the ingredients, pour into a glass and serve immediately

D

HEALTH STATISTICS
Apples are good for aiding digestion and provide the antioxidant quercetin and vitamin C, while the orange and lime provide additional vitamin C.

SHAKES

- Keep the fat content low by using skimmed milk or low-fat yoghurt in the recipes

- You may substitute soya milk or yoghurt, oat, rice or almond milk for the dairy version given in the recipes.

- For a thicker shake, add extra fruit (bananas produce the thickest creamiest consistency), crushed ice, or more yoghurt. If you use frozen fruit, the result will be a thicker drink.

- For maximum nutritional value and taste, drink your shake immediately.

BLUEBERRY YOGHURT SHAKE

M

HEALTH STATISTICS
Blueberries are super-rich sources of immunity-boosting vitamin C and antioxidants called anthocyanins. The bio-yoghurt provides protein, calcium and B-vitamins, and the live culture it contains helps promote a healthy gut.

MAKES 2 DRINKS
200 G (7 OZ) BLUEBERRIES
1 SMALL BANANA, PEELED AND SLICED
120 ML (4 FL OZ) APPLE JUICE
150 ML (5 FL OZ) NATURAL BIO-YOGHURT
CRUSHED ICE

Put the blueberries, banana, apple juice, bio-yoghurt and ice into a smoothie maker, blender or food processor and blend until smooth. Serve immediately.

RASPBERRY AND CRANBERRY SHAKE

MAKES 2 DRINKS
A CUPFUL OF CRUSHED ICE
250 ML (8 FL OZ) CRANBERRY AND RASPBERRY JUICE DRINK
125 G (4 OZ) RASPBERRIES
1 CARTON (150 G) NATURAL BIO-YOGHURT

Place the ice, cranberry juice, raspberries and yoghurt in the goblet of a smoothie maker, blender or food processor and process until the ingredients are thoroughly combined. Serve immediately.

HEALTH STATISTICS
Super-rich in vitamin C, this shake also provides powerful antioxidants that help your body fight off viruses and infections. Live yoghurt also boosts your immunity and improves the balance of beneficial bacteria in the gut.

MANGO AND GINGER SHAKE

MAKES 2 DRINKS
1 MANGO, PEELED, STONE REMOVED AND CUT INTO CHUNKS
A HANDFUL OF CRUSHED ICE
2 CM (1 IN) PIECE FRESH ROOT GINGER
250 ML (8 FL OZ) SKIMMED MILK OR NATURAL BIO-YOGHURT

Put the mango flesh, ice, ginger and milk or yoghurt into a smoothie maker, blender or food processor and blend until smooth. Serve immediately.

HEALTH STATISTICS
Mango is rich in betacarotene and vitamin C while the skimmed milk provides plenty of calcium and protein.

STRAWBERRY AND NECTARINE SHAKE

MAKES 2 DRINKS
A CUPFUL OF CRUSHED ICE
1 CARTON (150 ML) STRAWBERRY BIO-YOGHURT
6–8 STRAWBERRIES
1 NECTARINE, STONE REMOVED AND ROUGHLY CHOPPED
SKIMMED MILK

Put the ice, yoghurt, strawberries and nectarine in the goblet of a smoothie maker, blender or food processor and process until slushy. Adjust the consistency with skimmed milk. Serve immediately.

[M]

HEALTH STATISTICS
This nutritious shake is a terrific way of boosting your protein intake. It also provides good amounts of calcium, vitamin C, betacarotene and fibre.

STRAWBERRY BANANA SHAKE

MAKES 2 DRINKS
A CUPFUL OF CRUSHED ICE
125 G (4 OZ) STRAWBERRIES
200 ML (7 FL OZ) SKIMMED MILK
1 BANANA

Put the ice, strawberries, milk and banana in the goblet of a smoothie maker, blender or food processor and process until smooth. Adjust the consistency with milk, if necessary. Serve immediately.

[M]

HEALTH STATISTICS
Strawberries are super-rich in vitamin C and the banana provides additional fibre and potassium. The milk adds protein and calcium.

CHAPTER 12
DESSERTS

Contrary to popular myth, desserts need not be fattening. In fact, they can be positively healthy. Here seasonal fresh fruit, berries, exotic fruit and even dried fruit – rich in immunity-boosting vitamins and antioxidants – form the basis of mouth-watering salads, jellies, mousses, sorbets and crumbles. Enjoy!

ORANGE AND APRICOT SORBET

MAKES 4 SERVINGS
300 ML (1/2 PINT) WATER
125 G (4 OZ) SUGAR
3 TABLESPOONS (45 ML) LEMON JUICE
GRATED ZEST AND JUICE OF 1 LARGE ORANGE
400 G (14 OZ) FRESH APRICOTS, HALVED AND STONED
1 EGG WHITE

Put the water, sugar, lemon juice, orange zest and juice into a saucepan and bring to the boil, stirring until the sugar has dissolved. Boil rapidly for about 5 minutes. Add the apricots and simmer gently for 2 minutes. Leave to cool.

Pour the fruit and syrup into a food processor or blender and process to a smooth purée.

Pour into a container suitable for freezing, cover and freeze for about 2 hours until frozen around the sides. Alternatively, pour the mixture into an ice-cream machine and freeze until half-frozen.

Whisk the egg white until it forms soft peaks. If using an ice-cream maker add to the half-frozen mixture and continue freezing until completely frozen. Otherwise, tip the half-frozen mixture into a bowl and whisk briefly until smooth. Fold in the whisked egg white. Pour the mixture back into the container and freeze for about 6 hours.

Remove the sorbet from the freezer about 20 minutes before serving and transfer to the fridge.

M

HEALTH STATISTICS
This sorbet provides vitamin C from the pineapple and citrus juices, which helps boost immunity and protect against cancer and premature ageing.

APPLE AND APRICOT COMPOTE

MAKES 4 SERVINGS

125 G (4 OZ) DRIED ORGANIC APRICOTS (UNSULPHURED)
450 G (1 LB) APPLES, PEELED, CORED AND CHOPPED
1 TABLESPOON (15 ML) CLEAR HONEY
JUICE OF 1 LEMON
1/2–1 TEASPOON (2.5–5 ML) GROUND CINNAMON

Soak the apricots in a little hot water for at least 2 hours. Alternatively leave to soak in the fridge overnight.

Drain and chop the apricots.

Put the apples, honey, lemon juice and cinnamon in a saucepan. Add the apricots together with their soaking liquid. Stir and bring to the boil. Reduce the heat and simmer for 10 minutes until the fruit is just tender. Allow to cool.

Spoon the fruit mixture into 4 serving dishes.

Serve this compote with natural or Greek yoghurt and a drizzle of maple syrup.

HEALTH STATISTICS

Apples are rich in fibre, potassium and the flavanoid, quercetin, which has anticancer and anti-inflammatory actions. Dried apricots are rich in betacarotene and iron.

SPICED HUNZA APRICOT COMPOTE

MAKES 4 SERVINGS

250G (9 OZ) DRIED HUNZA APRICOTS
3–4 WHOLE CLOVES
3 SLICES OF FRESH GINGER, CRUSHED
2 ORANGES
1 TABLESPOON (15 ML) MAPLE SYRUP OR ACACIA HONEY
1 STICK OF CINNAMON
3–4 CARDAMOM PODS

Cover the apricots with about 500 ml (16 fl oz) hot water and leave to soak overnight.

Peel the oranges using a vegetable peeler. Divide the oranges into segments and roughly chop.

Place the orange peel, cloves, ginger, apricots and their soaking liquid in a saucepan. Add in the chopped orange, maple syrup or honey, cinnamon stick (snapped in half) and cardamom pods.

Bring to the boil and then turn down the heat to gently poach for 8–10 minutes until the apricots are softened. Allow to cool in the cooking liquid then divide into 4 individual bowls.

D

HEALTH STATISTICS
Dried apricots are rich in iron and betacarotene, a powerful antioxidant that combats premature ageing, heart disease and cancer.

RASPBERRY AND BLUEBERRY MOUSSE

MAKES 4 SERVINGS
125 G (4 OZ) BLUEBERRIES
225 G (8 OZ) RASPBERRIES
300 G (10 OZ) SILKEN TOFU
2 TABLESPOONS (30 ML) CLEAR HONEY

Reserve a few raspberries and blueberries for decoration. Place the remaining fruit in a blender or food processor with the tofu and honey. Blend until smooth. Divide into 4 individual dishes.

Decorate with the reserved fruit. Chill in the fridge and serve.

D

HEALTH STATISTICS
Blueberries are rich in phytonutrients and have the highest antioxidant capacity of all fresh fruit. Both blueberries and raspberries are rich in vitamin C. This dessert is also a good source of protein and calcium (from the tofu).

STRAWBERRY JELLY

MAKE 4 SERVINGS
1 HEAPED TABLESPOON (15 ML) AGAR-AGAR FLAKES
(OR 1 SACHET OF POWDERED AGAR-AGAR)
200 ML (7 FL OZ) WATER
400 ML (7 FL OZ) CRANBERRY AND RASPBERRY JUICE
250 G (9 OZ) FRESH OR FROZEN STRAWBERRIES

Mix together the agar-agar and water in a small saucepan. Bring to the boil, whisking continuously, reduce the heat and simmer for 4–5 minutes.

Add the fruit juice and mix together. Leave to cool.

Divide the strawberries between 4 glass dessert bowls and pour the cooled liquid jelly over to cover the fruit.

Chill in the fridge until set.

HEALTH STATISTICS
This vegetarian fresh-fruit jelly is packed with vitamin C, a powerful antioxidant and immune booster.

PINEAPPLE AND MANGO

MAKES 4 SERVINGS
1 RIPE PINEAPPLE
1 LARGE MANGO
2 LIMES
2 TEASPOONS (10 ML) CLEAR ACACIA HONEY

Peel the pineapple, cut into 1 cm (½ in) rounds then cut each round into quarters.

Slice through the mango either side of the stone. Peel, then cut the flesh into cubes.

Place the fruit in a serving bowl.

Finely grate the rind from the limes and add to the fruit. Squeeze the juice then put in a small saucepan with the acacia honey. Heat gently, stirring, just until the honey has dissolved. Allow to cool.

Pour the cooled lime juice over the fruit and toss well.

HEALTH STATISTICS
Mango is rich in betacarotene and vitamin C – both antioxidant nutrients – and pineapple also provides vitamin C.

APPLE AND RASPBERRY CRUMBLE

MAKES 4–6 SERVINGS
2 LARGE COOKING APPLES, PEELED, CORED AND SLICED
125 G (4 OZ) FRESH OR FROZEN RASPBERRIES
2 TABLESPOONS (30 ML) WATER
4 TABLESPOONS (60 ML) CLEAR HONEY
60 G (2OZ) FLAKED ALMONDS, CRUSHED
60 G (2 OZ) OATS
25 G (1 OZ) MILLET FLAKES
25 G (1 OZ) RICE FLOUR
60 G (2 OZ) DAIRY-FREE SPREAD

Preheat the oven to 190 C/ 375 F/ Gas mark 5.

Put the prepared apples, raspberries and water into an ovenproof dish. In a saucepan, melt 2 tablespoons (30 ml) of the honey with the water over a low heat. Pour over the fruit and mix together.

Place the flaked almonds, oats, rice flour, dairy-free spread and the remaining honey in a bowl and mix together with your fingers until you have a sticky crumb mixture. Alternatively, put in a food processor and pulse until the mixture forms fine crumbs.

Spread the oat crumble over the fruit and bake in the oven for about 25 minutes until the topping is golden. Do not overbake otherwise the topping will become too hard.

HEALTH STATISTICS
This dessert is rich in fibre and vitamin C (from the raspberries and apples). The almonds provide protein, calcium and heart-healthy monounsaturated oils, and the oats are rich in B-vitamins and soluble fibre which helps balance blood sugar levels.

THAI FRUIT SALAD

HALF A PINEAPPLE
HALF A HONEYDEW MELON
A QUARTER OF A WATERMELON
1 STAR FRUIT
60 G (2 OZ) COCONUT FLAKES (OR 125 G (4 OZ) FRESH COCONUT)
4 PASSION FRUIT
JUICE OF 2 LIMES

Peel the pineapple and cut into quarters. Cut out and discard the tough inner core. Cut each quarter lengthwise then slice across into chunks.

Scoop out the seeds from the honeydew melon, cut into slices, peel and slice into chunks.

Cut the watermelon into chunks, discarding skin and any seeds.

Cut the star fruit into four, and then slice finely.

In a large bowl toss together the pineapple, honeydew melon, watermelon, star fruit and coconut. Halve the passion fruits and scoop out their pulp into a separate bowl. Mix in the lime juice, then pour over the mixed fruit, and toss together. Cover and chill until serving.

D

HEALTH STATISTICS
This fruit salad is rich in vitamin C, potassium and fibre. Watermelon is also rich in lycopene, an antioxidant that helps prevent cancer of the stomach, colon and prostate.

PLUMS WITH ORANGE AND MINT

MAKES 4 SERVINGS

450 G (1 LB) PURPLE PLUMS
125 G (4 FL OZ) FRESH ORANGE JUICE
1 TABLESPOON (15 ML) CHOPPED FRESH MINT LEAVES
A LITTLE HONEY OR MAPLE SYRUP (OPTIONAL)

Halve the plums and remove the stones. Cut them into thin slices and place in a bowl.

Add the remaining ingredients and toss well.

Cover and chill in the fridge, stirring occasionally, for at least 2 hours.

HEALTH STATISTICS
Plums are a good source of fibre and have antioxidant benefits. They contain hydroxycinnamic acid, which is associated with a reduced risk of colon cancer.

FRESH FRUIT WITH HONEY, MINT AND LIME

JUICE AND ZEST OF 2 LIMES
2 TABLESPOONS (30 ML) ACACIA HONEY
2 TABLESPOONS (30 ML) CHOPPED FRESH MINT
1 CANTALOUPE MELON, HALVED AND SEEDED
350 G (12 OZ) STRAWBERRIES, HULLED AND HALVED
4 KIWI FRUIT, PEELED, CUT INTO 1/2-INCH PIECES
125 G (4 OZ) SEEDLESS GRAPES

Whisk lime juice and zest, honey and mint in large bowl to blend.

Using melon baller or spoon, scoop out cantaloupe.

Add all the fruit to the honey syrup in the bowl. Toss to combine. Let it stand for 15 minutes to allow the flavours to blend. Cover and chill until you are ready to serve.

D

HEALTH STATISTICS
Cantaloupe melon is super-rich in betacarotene, an antioxidant linked to a reduced risk of cancer and heart disease. Strawberries and lime juice are super-rich in vitamin C, another powerful antioxidant with proven health benefits.

MELON AND STRAWBERRIES

MAKES 4 SERVINGS
1 CANTALOUPE MELON
225 G (8 OZ) STRAWBERRIES
GRATED ZEST AND JUICE OF 1 LIME
150 ML (5 FL OZ) APPLE JUICE
1 TABLESPOON (15 ML) CHOPPED FRESH MINT

Remove the seeds from the melon. Cut the flesh into bite-sized pieces or scoop out with a melon baller.

Wash, hull and halve the strawberries.

Combine the prepared fruit with the lime zest and juice and apple juice in a large bowl. Just before serving, stir in the chopped fresh mint.

This dessert is delicious served on its own or with a dollop of Greek yoghurt or crème fraîche.

HEALTH STATISTICS
Cantaloupe melon is super-rich in betacarotene, and strawberries and limes are super-rich in vitamin C. Both are powerful anticancer nutrients.